"Thanks to *Making Spiritual Progress*, our church community has greater faith, hope, love, accountability and community."
Barry Sappington, lead pastor, Crosspointe Life Church

"Allen Ratta's insight will help you in what is a lifelong pursuit: growing. Read and continue the journey of developing. *Making Spiritual Progress* is a book that will enlighten your path."
Johnny Hunt, former president, Southern Baptist Convention

"For the leader who recognizes that lifelong learning and growth are keys to leadership health and longevity, Allen's insights are both helpful and encouraging."
Les Welk, superintendent, Northwest Ministry Network of the Assemblies of God

"Most of us spend time trying to fix our behaviors. What we need is something that will change us from the inside out, down to our very DNA. *Making Spiritual Progress* will help you to achieve spiritual growth."
Greg Surratt, author of *Ir-rev-rend*

"Allan Ratta has remarkable insight into what it means to experience real and lasting spiritual transformation, and the ability to lead people into it. His commitment to seeing people become their true selves is contagious. Read this book with an open heart and you will find there is no going back to a life without meaning and purpose."
Terry Crist, senior pastor, City of Grace, Phoenix

"*Making Spiritual Progress* is about changing our lives, starting with our motives. When we are motivated by faith, hope and love, our behaviors will fall into line. Allen Ratta shows us how to change lives, starting with the heart."
Josh Hunt, author of *Good Questions Have Groups Talking*

"Personal and probing, *Making Spiritual Progress* will provide practical and applicable principles that will change your spiritual journey and give strength to fulfill your call."
James R. Braddy, superintendent, Northern California/Nevada District of the Assemblies of God

"*Making Spiritual Progress* is the culmination of Allen's lifelong pursuit of spiritual growth written through the lens of practicality, life experience as a pastor, but most importantly, the leading of the Holy Spirit."
Gary Morefield, pastor, GV Christian, Henderson, Nevada

"Instead of discipleship being the end game, Allen demonstrates how discipleship is the means to the ultimate goal of developing our faith, strengthening our hope and increasing our love for God and others. Want to make progress in your spiritual journey? Read this book."
Jim Tomberlin, author of *Better Together*

"Zeroing in on our hearts and motivations, Allen Ratta diagnoses the critical factors that often block our spiritual transformation. . . . In this compelling volume you'll find biblical and practical information to be able to assimilate for growing in grace and truth!"
Rich Guerra, superintendent, SoCal Network Assemblies of God

"Allen Ratta has a unique and effective grace to communicate insights regarding faith, hope and love. The truths he unveils will brighten the path for anyone—from parent to pastor—to receive and minister genuine transformation."
Kimberly Dirman, southwest district supervisor, Foursquare Church

"We are always on the lookout for quality discipleship materials. After reading the first three chapters of Allen's book I told our staff I had discovered a gold mine! Faith, hope and love are the foundational virtues that grow a person in Christ. I hope every church and pastor will take a look at this material for their church."
Hal Seed, pastor, New Song Community Church, Oceanside, California

"*Making Spiritual Progress* causes the reader to look deeply within, exposing the mysteries of Christ's gospel in and through each of us. This work is a paradigm-shifting road to an encounter with Christ that changes hearts, changes lives, changes ministries."
Joseph Girdler, superintendent, Kentucky Ministry Network of the Assemblies of God

"With a beguiling simplicity, Alan weaves a story about our behaviors, our character and our motivations. At each point he weaves Scripture and modern-day stories to point us to a focused way of thinking and living."
David Fletcher, founder and host, Xpastor

MAKING SPIRITUAL PROGRESS

Building Your Life with
Faith, Hope and Love

ALLEN RATTA

IVP Books

An imprint of InterVarsity Press
Downers Grove, Illinois

InterVarsity Press
P.O. Box 1400, Downers Grove, IL 60515-1426
World Wide Web: www.ivpress.com
Email: email@ivpress.com

InterVarsity Press® is the book-publishing division of InterVarsity Christian Fellowship/USA®, a movement of students and faculty active on campus at hundreds of universities, colleges and schools of nursing in the United States of America, and a member movement of the International Fellowship of Evangelical Students. For information about local and regional activities, write Public Relations Dept., InterVarsity Christian Fellowship/USA, 6400 Schroeder Rd., P.O. Box 7895, Madison, WI 53707-7895, or visit the IVCF website at www.intervarsity.org.

All Scripture quotations, unless otherwise indicated, are taken from the New American Standard Bible®, copyright 1960, 1962, 1963, 1968, 1971, 1972, 1973, 1975, 1977, 1995 by The Lockman Foundation. Used by permission.

While all stories in this book are true, some names and identifying information in this book have been changed to protect the privacy of the individuals involved.

Cover design: Cindy Kiple
Interior design: Beth Hagenberg
Images: © Stefanie Timmermann/iStockphoto

ISBN 978-0-8308-4405-0 (print)
ISBN 978-0-8308-6499-7 (digital)

Printed in the United States of America ∞

Library of Congress Cataloging-in-Publication Data

A catalog record for this book is available from the Library of Congress.

P	17	16	15	14	13	12	11	10	9	8	7	6	5	4	3	2	1
Y	29	28	27	26	25	24	23	22	21	20	19	18	17	16	15	14

CONTENTS

FOREWORD

Faith, Hope and Love. Three simple but profound words. They're deep. They're life changing. But let's be honest. For anyone who has been a Christian for a long time, these three words are also so familiar they can become white noise, spiritual clichés—reduced to the level of meaningless Christianese.

That's incredibly unfortunate, because Faith, Hope and Love aren't Christian clichés. They're the stuff of spiritual maturity: the ground floor, infrastructure and scaffolding that the Holy Spirit uses to make us more like Jesus.

In *Making Spiritual Progress* Allen Ratta digs deep into the important role that each of these three virtues plays in our spiritual growth. What the early church leaders called "cardinal virtues" he calls "motivational virtues."

But this is not a book about willpower. It's a book about alignment.

When it comes to spiritual progress, willpower won't cut it. Our flesh can never do the work of the Spirit. Granted, with self-discipline we can make changes. We can tack on new behaviors and stop doing other behaviors. But those kinds of changes are exhausting—and almost always temporary. They're hard to pull off and even harder to maintain. Worse, they can deceive us into thinking that we've actually changed ourselves on the inside, that a cosmetic change equals a heart change. It's as if we've fastened fresh oranges onto a couple of tree stumps and started to believe that we've created an orange grove.

But what willpower can't do, God will do. It all starts with what the Bible calls yielding to the Holy Spirit—aligning our motivations, values and thoughts with the Scriptures and the Spirit's inner promptings.

The fact is, our behavior flows naturally and almost effortlessly out of our core motivations. We can't help but live in light of them. That's why whenever our actions seem to conflict with our values, it's a telltale sign that our *stated* values and motivations are different from our *core* values and motivation. And it's why spiritual transformation always begins with a renewed mind that realigns our thoughts, motivations and values with God's will and Word.

And that's where Faith, Hope and Love come in. They're incredibly important foundational spiritual indicators. Whenever they're absent or weak, we'll end up living selfishly, making self-centered decisions that lead to spiritually destructive behavior and dire consequences. But as we grow in Faith, Hope and Love, we'll end up living for Jesus and others, making Spirit-led decisions that lead to Spirit-led behavior resulting in the experience of God's good, pleasing and perfect will.

That's why Ratta claims that our personal spiritual progress can often be measured with one simple question: *How am I growing in Faith, in Hope and in Love?*

I believe he is right. The Spiritual Progress model fits so well with the biblical paradigm that it's almost a priori obvious, once you step back and look at it. It makes you wonder, *Why hadn't I seen that before?*

As you read through this book, you'll discover the motivational power that each of these three virtues has on our lives, and how our response to each one impacts our spiritual progress for either good or bad.

You'll also find that Ratta goes beyond mere theory. He offers practical steps that anyone can take. He helps us honestly access where we are in terms of Faith, Hope and Love, and he offers practical and biblical steps to help us grow in each area.

Whether your spiritual life is steadily moving forward, merely treading water or about to go under, I believe the insights in this book will help you to become more like Jesus. That's because at the end of the day, any time we submit to God's Word and more carefully realign our values and motivations with his, spiritual progress is inevitable. And any time we don't, it's impossible.

Larry Osborne
author and pastor, North Coast Church, Vista, CA

1

THE FIVE RULES OF PERSONAL MOTIVATION

Understanding Our Motivations

> *When all is said and done,*
> *more is said than done.*
>
> Lou Holtz

> *When he comes,*
> *he will bring out in the open . . .*
> *all kinds of things we never even dreamed of—*
> *inner motives and purposes. . . . Only*
> *then will any one of us get to*
> *hear the "Well done!"*
>
> 1 Corinthians 4:5, *The Message*

Have you ever asked yourself, "Why in the world did I do that?"

Everyone, at one time or another, has regretted something they said or did. A friend recently confided, "Sometimes it seems as if I am observing someone else when I do certain things. Like a mysterious inner force has taken over my body." This sounds a lot like the ancient words of Paul as he candidly revealed his own personal struggles: "For what I am doing, I do not understand; for I am not practicing what I would like to do, but I am doing the very thing I hate" (Romans 7:15).

His words, "I do not understand," make perfect sense to us two thousand years later. The truth is that there *are* mysterious forces at work behind the scenes that can cause us to act out in ways that are counter to our wishes, convictions and sensibilities. These forces are called motivations, and they determine the outcome of our lives.

This is a book about understanding and managing our motivations.

THE HEART IS ALWAYS MOTIVATED

God has so constructed the human heart that it is *always* fully motivated. "This cannot be true!" you counter. "I see people, including myself, who struggle with a lack of motivation all the time."

Let's look at some examples. Take the case of the incessant dieter who struggles with obesity as he stealthily sneaks another forbidden delicacy. What about failing students who cannot bring themselves to study? Consider Christians who yearn for greater spiritual intimacy but fail to practice consistent spiritual disciplines. Think about the homeless derelict on the street corner, holding a disingenuous sign that says, "Will work for food!" Or what about the individual who won't even get up to hold a sign? "Surely these people lack motivation!" you say.

Wrong. The people on this list are all highly motivated individuals. The problem is that they are more highly motivated to stay where they are than to change. The dieter is more motivated by the taste of the rich, creamy sweetness of a cream puff than by the ego boost of wearing a smaller pair of jeans. The student is more motivated by the joys of social discovery than by a chance to qualify for entry to a top-flight college. The Christian is more motivated by the immediacy of the flesh than by the delights of spiritual discovery. A homeless man will cling to his fierce desire for independence at the expense of having a roof over his head. Motivated people, like the apostle Paul, sometimes find themselves doing the "very thing" they "hate."

Motivations are the energies that propel us and drive the decisions we make. They are the substance of our character. All behaviors stem from an underlying motivation. Motivations are the invisible, unstoppable forces that can lift us to greatness or plunge us to utter ruin.

It is true that with enough willpower you may succeed in changing your outward conduct for a season. But if the underlying motivational condition of the heart stays the same, it will surely reassert its power. Pounds will return. Grades will lower. Spiritual vitality will wane.

Motivations are not to be confused with good intentions or willpower. Our intentions, no matter how noble or determined, lack the driving force to transform our lives. The world would be a far different place if our wishes were effective at altering our behaviors.

How can we achieve our highest aspirations? Positive change *automatically* happens when our hearts are captivated and energized by the *right* motivation. The path to changing our actions begins when we take the time to understand the powerful motivational currents that reside, in many cases, just beneath the threshold of our conscious minds.

THE BEHAVIORAL SUPPLY CHAIN

Our actions do not occur in isolation; rather, a number of sources work to bring a behavior to fruition. Think of it like a can of beans on a store shelf. The beans did not magically arrive there one day. There was a long supply chain involved. Major investments were made to buy the seed, prepare the soil, plant the beans, water the soil, and fertilize and harvest the beans, which were then sent to a cannery. They entered a distribution network before they could finally arrive on your local grocery store shelf.

The same is true of our behaviors. They do not magically arrive on the scene one day. They have been "on the way" for a long time. The

pipeline is full, so they can show up at a moment's notice. It is silly
to blame circumstances or someone else for the way we act. The truth
is that we have been incubating our behaviors for a long time. For the
remainder of this chapter we will illustrate, one by one, the elements
involved in our behavioral supply chain. These are the factors that
motivate us to do what we do.

THE FIRST RULE OF PERSONAL MOTIVATION:
The Principle of Cause and Effect
Our behaviors flow naturally and effortlessly out of our character.

Cause and effect is uniformly embedded throughout creation.
Jesus spotlighted it when he compared human nature to the natural
world: "So every good tree bears good fruit, but the bad tree bears bad
fruit. A good tree cannot produce bad fruit, nor can a bad tree
produce good fruit" (Matthew 7:17-18).

Your character, like the DNA of a tree, determines the nature of
your fruit. The coding runs so deep that nothing can be done to
change this cause-and-effect reality. Your character consists of a habitual mix and intensity of motivations. Your character sets the course
for how you are going to conduct yourself as you move through life.
Figure 1.1 illustrates this impact.

5 FACTORS THAT DETERMINE OUR BEHAVIORS – FACTOR #1
Our **Behaviors** (ARE PREDETERMINED BY) ← Our **CHARACTER**

Figure 1.1

Effortlessness. It is easy and natural to act out in ways that are
consistent with the kind of person that you are on the inside. Jesus'
words *"every good tree bears good fruit"* state a simple fact. There
are no exceptions. Good behaviors flow effortlessly from good character. Apple trees never sweat trying to make apples. Their fruit is
a natural consequence of who they are on the inside.

Think of all the anxiety, hard work and frustration people go through trying to change themselves from the *outside* in! Entire industries are built upon the desire that people have to transform their lives. Motivational speakers peddle their wares in front of the hopeful masses. All of this frenzied activity goes on in spite of the fact that "fruit changing" is a failed approach. There must be an easier way.

Consistency. It is senseless to expect a person to act consistently different from who they are on the inside. People inevitably act out in ways that expose the nature of their "tree." Thorn bushes, no matter how hard they may try, can never produce apples.

Jesus drew a firm line in the sand when he said, "nor can a bad tree produce good fruit." If we stopped right here, things would appear hopeless for the bad tree. You are what you are! If you have bad motivations, they produce bad character and your bad character will keep you behaving badly. We see this destructive cycle in the lives of people all around us. Is it possible for a person with bad character to change their fruit? Evidently not! But don't give up hope. Jesus established another way.

Tree changing. Jesus revisits the tree metaphor a few chapters later in the book of Matthew and reveals a greater and incredibly liberating truth about human nature: "Either *make the tree good* and its fruit good, or make the tree bad and its fruit bad; for the tree is known by its fruit" (Matthew 12:33).

"*Make the tree.*" What a concept! "Tree making" introduces an entirely new approach to personal growth. If you can't change your fruit, then change your tree! Having a "good tree" means that you will not have to worry about bad fruit. Good trees naturally produce good fruit. In this verse Jesus introduces the possibility for radical, transformational change. It begins on the inside and works its way outward into our relationships with our self and others.

Contrast this with every worldly method for self-improvement. They fixate on "fruit changing"—that is, changing your *outward* behaviors. The Creator calls this a colossal waste of time and energy. Transformation begins when we understand and obey the command, "Make the tree good . . . or make the tree bad." Jesus leaves no room for any middle ground, or he would have said, "Make the tree better."

The words *make the tree good* are some of the most hope-filled words in the Bible. The implications are mind-boggling! They mean that I can do far more than just change some of my behaviors. *I can become an entirely new person!* A thorn bush can be supernaturally transformed into an apple tree. Jesus did not come to give you a better life but to give you a new life. We will explore in great detail, at a later point, *how* a person can make their tree good. The possibilities for personal growth have now become endless.

Fruit inspections. Melissa was constantly bothered by the way her husband, Bob, acted. Everyone at church who was within earshot of Melissa knew all about her many grievances. Melissa disregarded the wise counsel of those around her and continued to unleash a daily tirade of brutal and degrading criticisms on her husband. Bob, who had a passive personality, eventually began to experience panic attacks. Melissa's criticisms only increased in their severity. Then it all came to a sudden end. In a deep state of depression Bob shot himself at the age of twenty-eight. Melissa wept bitterly as I conducted the funeral. She served as an unforgettable reminder of how toxic we can be in our attempts to change the behaviors of others.

It is easy to get caught up with how people *act*, or what has been called "fruit inspecting." The closer someone is to us, the more emotionally vested this activity becomes. When we see our spouse or our children acting in ways that trouble us, we feel a compelling urge to confront the behavior. Sometimes this is a healthy part of accountability. Often it is counterproductive meddling. We are kidding ourselves if we think that endlessly inspecting and chiding behaviors will bring about the kinds of changes we want to see. "Fruit fixation" is a failed path. You have Jesus' Word on it.

Successful interventions. The way to constructively deal with those who are misbehaving or underperforming requires an entirely different tack. Anger is a natural reaction to the way some people act, but anger does not change lives. God has called us to move beyond anger in our relationships. Love has learned to pause and ask a deeply meaningful question: "Why are they doing that?" Outward actions are always symptoms of much deeper issues. If your child or spouse has any real hope to change and grow, it will require a treatment regimen that goes far deeper than addressing their visible behaviors. If you desire to be a helpful change agent, you will need to gain true insights into *why* people do what they do. Effective life coaching must always penetrate to the level of one's motivations.

The same is true regarding our own behaviors. Personal growth begins when we ask a basic question about ourselves: "Why do I do what I do?" The answers to this question lead us down the only true path toward personal transformation.

THE SECOND RULE OF PERSONAL MOTIVATION:
The Principle of Simplicity
Our character is shaped by three fundamental motivations.

If God genuinely exists and if God is committed to our highest good (this book presumes both to be true on the basis of the Scriptures), it only makes sense that he would be in the motivational business. God knows we need all the positive motivation we can get! No motivational speaker you have ever heard has the ability to motivate you as positively or powerfully as God.

What is his unique approach to motivation? How does God move us toward our highest potential? What power does he use to shape our character?

God's motivational effectiveness is based on his intimate knowledge of how we were made to function. He has designed the human heart to be captivated by, filled with and transformed by three positive

energies—Faith, Hope and Love. God has established these motivational forces for our welfare. These are the currents by which God
picks us up, carries us along and helps us to arrive at our desired loca-
tions in life.

Our motivations are the shaping forces behind our character and,
as we have learned, our character determines our behavior (see figure
1.2). Our motivations explain, on an even deeper level, why we end
up doing what we do.

---

5 FACTORS THAT DETERMINE OUR BEHAVIORS – FACTOR #2

Our Behaviors ← Our **Character** (IS PREDETERMINED BY) Our **MOTIVATIONS**

Figure 1.2

A strong case can be made from the Bible that Faith, Hope and Love
are the *only* positive forces that have this kind of motivational power to
shape our character. Early church leaders called them the Cardinal
Virtues, embracing their special role. "But now faith, hope, love, abide
these three; but the greatest of these is love" (1 Corinthians 13:13).

If it is true that there are only three "positive motivational forces"
in the world (we shall establish this as a matter of fact in the current
and subsequent chapter), then the ability to improve our "self" becomes a greatly simplified matter. Instead of trying to achieve lots
of desirable behavioral traits, my focus becomes much more
limited. I get to concentrate on just three things that have the
power to really change my life. My personal progress can be measured with one simple question: *How am I growing in Faith, in
Hope and in Love?*

The wonderful simplicity of the spiritual life. Tom was new to our
church. Not long after his arrival, he made an appointment and arrived at my office with a faded yellow notepad clutched tightly in his
hand. I could not help but notice the disturbed look on his face as I
invited him to sit down on the brown overstuffed chair across from

my desk. I had learned from some earlier conversations that Tom was an intensely dedicated Christian.

"Pastor," he sighed, with tears gathering in his eyes, "Christianity is just not working for me anymore." He held up the tattered notebook to reveal that the first page was completely filled with a long list of words. His story tumbled out as if compressed in a deep oil well. He had accumulated two huge personal growth lists from several years of listening to sermons, reading the Bible and observing people. One list recorded the eighty-seven desirable behavioral traits that he wanted in his life. The other list comprised fifty-four negative traits that he wanted to avoid. At the end of every day he would review his lists to see how well he was doing.

"Tom," I interjected with compassion filling my heart, "that kind of Christianity would not work for me either." I took a deep breath and continued, "Just looking at your first page makes me weary. This is not the way Jesus intended for you or anybody to live."

I started the process that day of introducing Tom to the wonderful simplicity of the spiritual life. Much of what I shared with him is written in these pages. I am happy to report that Tom learned to embrace a spiritual path that has transformed his life and filled him with joy on the journey.

Motivational power. Faith, Hope and Love are the three motivational fountainheads from which a multitude of good and positive behaviors naturally flow. Trying to change our behaviors in a direction that runs counter to our motivations is a failed strategy. The ways that we act are merely symptomatic of our underlying motivations. Sadly, I see many Toms out there who spend vast energies addressing their surface issues while ignoring the root causes behind their actions. Treating our symptoms may make us feel better for a short while, but we need a soul cure that goes much deeper.

Our behaviors are predetermined by our character. How can this insight help us? What do I need to know about my character to change my behaviors? We can learn three primary lessons from observing the created nature of fruit trees—effortlessness, consistency and tree changing.

A Faith-filled, Hope-filled and Love-filled heart will always produce noticeably positive behaviors. They push us in specific directions and motivate us to act in highly predictable ways: Faith trusts; Hope endures; Love gives.

The opposite pattern can be observed in those who are very low in Faith, Hope and Love. A person's behavior can always be associated with one of these primary underlying motivations. With some biblical insight and a little practice, anyone can gain the ability to discern many of the underlying motivations of those around them. Knowing why people do what they do will significantly improve your interpersonal and people-management skills.

Before we rush ahead to investigate the motivational power of Faith, Hope and Love, let's take an important pause to look at the remaining three rules of personal motivation.

Faith, Hope and Love are the most highly charged motivational conditions of the human spirit. I call them the *Motivational Virtues*. They encompass the entirety and the beautiful simplicity of the spiritual life. A person needs to look no further to understand why they do what they do.

THE THIRD RULE OF PERSONAL MOTIVATION:
The Principle of Captivation

Motivations naturally develop to serve the lord that rules us.

The human heart is constructed in such a way that makes it naturally susceptible to the outside rule of someone or something. We are, by nature, programmed to be in relationship with, to be subject to and to worship an authority greater than us. This notion of dependency, or what one might call subservience to a higher power, is highly offensive to the modern mind. We like to imagine that we are capable of being entirely in charge of our own lives. This kind of thinking is self-deception at its basest level.

What happens when we choose self-rule? Power abhors a vacuum. In the absence of our rightful Sovereign's rule, someone or something will ascend to the throne of our lives and make us its captive. This principle is true even when we have convinced ourselves that we are living freely and are the master of our souls. We have now entered the realm of compulsive behaviors and addictions.

Divine design. There is a great deal of worldly evidence that proves how poorly we function at self-governance. For starters, look at the level of pain in the world that would not exist without the negative behavior of people. Self-rule inevitably ends up hurting ourselves and hurting others. Why? The specifications that God used when he created people did not include the following:

- Must be wise enough to see all factors everywhere so as to never make a bad decision

- Must be able to see into the future to know the end of a matter when acting in the present

- Must be impervious to sin, so as to always exercise perfect love and goodness toward self and others, resulting in complete trustworthiness

- Must be all-powerful so as to never succumb to attractions or addictions, and be able to operate independently as a self-governing sovereign in the universe

Why not create humanity with these kinds of attributes? The Creator did not need any more masters of the universe. One is enough. God is powerful enough, good enough and loving enough to be our trusted friend, navigator and governor for life.

The truth goes deeper. You can *only* have *one* sovereign in the universe. The alternative is as ugly as the world in which we live. Wars, conflicts, fights and turmoil of every kind are the inevitable consequence of a universe filled with many sovereigns battling for control. Lasting peace only exists when the matter of dominion is clearly established.

God's rightful rule. Let's look at two major themes that emerge from the narrative of the Bible. First is the story about God's love for humankind and his desire to fellowship (become friends) with us. The end of the Bible offers a closing heartfelt appeal from Christ: "Look! I stand at the door and knock. If you hear my voice and open the door, I will come in, and we will share a meal together as friends" (Revelation 3:20 NLT). Second, the Bible begins with the story of the rebellion of Adam and Eve and culminates with the reestablishment of God's rightful rule over humanity: "So that at the name of Jesus every knee will bow, of those who are in heaven and on earth and under the earth, and that every tongue will confess that Jesus Christ is Lord, to the glory of God the Father" (Philippians 2:10-11).

Why is the establishment of God's dominion in one's heart so critical? The path to inner peace requires that all the usurpers to God's dominion be defeated. This is why God does more than just invite us into a personal relationship with him; he wants to establish his rightful rule over us. God's invitation for friendship is bundled within the context of his kingdom. "Seek first His kingdom" (Matthew 6:33) is more than just a suggestion—it is the only way to live a life that is free from everything that would otherwise ensnare us.

It is important to add that, under the right circumstances, we can be glorious. When we are operating under the lordship of Christ, his authority can be powerfully manifested through us. I saw wonderful evidence of this in the small group that my wife and I attend. A woman who is normally meek in her demeanor shared an incident where she spiritually impacted a stranger. Her face lit up as she recounted how she "felt God's power" and "spoke boldly," all the while wondering where the words were coming from that flowed out of her mouth. Jesus talked about this kind of divine empowerment: "Do not worry beforehand about what you are to say, but say whatever is given you in that hour; for it is not you who speak, but it is the Holy Spirit" (Mark 13:11).

Since Christ is our rightful Lord, it's readily apparent that we were designed to be followers. This inherent design is why we are so highly susceptible to negative forces, lusts and addictions when we operate outside the lordship of Christ. Peter exposed our vulnerability: "For by what a man is overcome, by this he is enslaved" (2 Peter 2:19). The lordship of Christ presents us with a clear fork in the road. Upon which path will we set our course? Whom will we follow? Who will be our master? A choice *must* be made. No choice is still making a choice. Jesus used language that leaves no room for compromise. "No one can serve two masters; for either he will hate the one and love the other, or he will be devoted to one and despise the other. You cannot serve God and wealth" (Matthew 6:24).

Our motivations will eventually conform to the demands of the master that establishes dominion over us. We can now illustrate another component in the progression of elements that lead to the way we act. Our behavior is predetermined by our character. Our character is determined by our motivations. Our motivations work to serve our master.

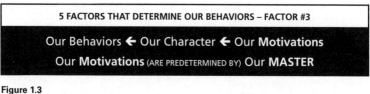

5 FACTORS THAT DETERMINE OUR BEHAVIORS – FACTOR #3

Our Behaviors ← Our Character ← Our **Motivations**
Our **Motivations** (ARE PREDETERMINED BY) Our **MASTER**

Figure 1.3

THE FOURTH RULE OF PERSONAL MOTIVATION:
The Heart-Centric Principle

All motivations, good or evil, reside in the heart.

The ancient wisdom of Solomon remains true: "Watch over your heart with all diligence, for from it flow the springs of life" (Proverbs

4:23). We must get to the level of the *heart* if we are to gain the ability to manage our motivations.

Take note! The Bible does *not* warn us to "be careful what you do" or "be careful what you say." This is the typical religious approach. The Bible, however, directs our attention inward, to the one area that matters most. *Be careful of your heart.*

The heart is the home turf where motivations compete for dominion, where the claims for sovereignty over our will are won or lost. We can now add another element to our illustration of why we do what we do: Your behavior is predetermined by your character. Your character is determined by your motivations. Your motivations grow to serve your master. Your heart determines which master you will follow.

---

5 FACTORS THAT DETERMINE OUR BEHAVIORS – FACTOR #4

Our Behaviors ← Our Character ← Our Motivations
Our **Master** (IS PREDETERMINED BY) Our **HEART**

Figure 1.4

Once we understand the ultimate source for our behaviors, we are far more prepared to expend our energies in ways that make a difference. How pointless it is to fervently wage war on the way that we act! The chances for victory are not good when we are chasing mere symptoms, far from the front lines.

When we ask, "Why in the world did I do that?" it is a good time to ask another deep question: "What is going on inside my heart?" Behaviors are always a matter of the heart.

Jesus taught, "Where your treasure is, there your heart will be also" (Matthew 6:21). What is meant by the word *treasure*? Your treasure consists of those things that you value the most. It may have nothing to do with gold, silver or the size of your financial nest egg. Ask yourself what kinds of yearnings occupy your thoughts. For some it is the pursuit of money. For others it may be the lust of bodily pleasures.

Still others may be driven by a desperate need for personal recognition and significance.

Treasure both *captivates* and *energizes* our hearts. At our core we are all treasure hunters. That is why the Bible warns us: "Do not store up for yourselves treasures on earth, where moth and rust destroy, and where thieves break in and steal. But store up for yourselves treasures in heaven, where neither moth nor rust destroys, and where thieves do not break in or steal" (Matthew 6:19-20).

The heart becomes attracted, captured and even addicted to certain treasures. These treasures seduce us and build loyalties to false masters that destroy and diminish our character. The allegiance of our hearts sets in motion a series of consequences that end up having a huge impact on the ways that we act. "The good man out of the good treasure of his heart brings forth what is good; and the evil man out of the evil treasure brings forth what is evil; for his mouth speaks from that which fills his heart" (Luke 6:45). If we are going to change our lives then some treasure swapping is in order.

Why do people like Melissa spew out poison and negativity? Why do people spin things in such a way as to elevate themselves at your expense? Why do people say hurtful things? We now have the answer: "for his *mouth speaks* from that which *fills his heart*." Planet earth is in desperate need of positively motivated hearts.

THE FIFTH RULE OF PERSONAL MOTIVATION:
The Principle of Indwelling

"My counsel is this: Live freely, animated and motivated by God's Spirit. Then you won't feed the compulsions of selfishness" (Galatians 5:16 *The Message*).

The Motivational Virtues of Faith, Hope and Love are unlike anything on earth. They are foreign to the way we naturally think. This is to be expected for they are not of this earth; they are spiritual.

Where do they come from? What is their source? They are the

direct result of God's activity in our lives. They flow through the indwelling of God's Spirit. They are gifts from God to us.

Consider the motivational virtue of Love. Love that flows from God's Spirit is far different from any kind of earthly or soul love you will ever experience. According to the Bible this Love is the most powerful force you could ever encounter: "For love is as strong as death. . . . Its flashes are flashes of fire, The very flame of the LORD" (Song of Solomon 8:6).

This otherworldly kind of Love transforms our thoughts and actions. It motivates us, by nature, to put the welfare of others ahead of self. It annihilates the timeless plague of self-centeredness. It has the power to transform any marriage and every significant relationship.

We need to understand more about Faith, Hope and Love if they are to bloom to their potential. How do they operate? How can I foster their development in my life?

Faith, Hope and Love are located in the heart. The heart is the soil where they bloom and bear fruit. We must become far more attuned to what is going on inside of us if we are to set our feet on the path of sustained personal growth.

Faith, Hope and Love come alive through the indwelling presence of God's Spirit. The Spirit is the ultimate power source for positive motivations. Personal growth requires that we put ourselves in a place of awareness where we are capable of hearing and responding to the movement of the Spirit.

The Spirit-Filled Heart	
Virtue	**Bible Verse**
Faith	"To be strengthened with power through His Spirit in the inner man, so that Christ may dwell in your hearts through faith." Ephesians 3:16-17
Hope	"May give to you a spirit of wisdom and of revelation in the knowledge of Him. I pray that the eyes of your heart may be enlightened, so that you will know what is the hope of His calling." Ephesians 1:17-18
Love	"The love of God has been poured out within our hearts through the Holy Spirit." Romans 5:5

Figure 1.5

The proactive agenda of the Spirit is proof that God is fervently committed to infuse us with positive motivations. It is God's intention that we become showcases of his goodness to a dark world. Jesus encouraged us to be God's goodness on display: "You are the light of the world. A city set on a hill cannot be hidden. . . . Let your light shine before men in such a way that they may see your good works, and glorify your Father who is in heaven" (Matthew 5:14, 16).

A wonderful confidence comes from understanding that God is constantly at work to better our lives. The apostle Paul summarized God's activity: he wants us to be "strengthened with power through His Spirit" (Ephesians 3:16; see figure 1.5).

We can now add the final element to the forces that explain our behaviors: Your behavior is predetermined by your character. Your character is determined by your motivations. Your motivations grow to serve your master. Your heart determines which master you follow. God's Spirit liberates our hearts to follow God.

---

5 FACTORS THAT DETERMINE OUR BEHAVIORS – FACTOR #5

Our Behaviors ← Our Character ← Our Motivations
Our Master ← Our **Heart** (IS LIBERATED BY) The **HOLY SPIRIT**

Figure 1.6

When you look at the progression of forces behind the ways that we act, it is painfully clear that "behaviors" can never be the starting point for personal growth. There are deep enduring reasons that explain our actions. In the coming chapters we will thoroughly explore the·underlying motivations for why we do what we do.

2

THE THREE GREAT FORCES OF POSITIVE MOTIVATION

The Engines of Transformation

> *You are never too old to set another*
> *goal or to dream a new dream.*
>
> C. S. Lewis

> *But now faith, hope,*
> *love, abide these three;*
> *but the greatest of*
> *these is love.*
>
> 1 Corinthians 13:13

How well is life working for you? Do you feel stuck in a reality that is less than you had hoped for? Are there some things about yourself or those who are closest to you that repeatedly bum you out? Do you believe in a vision of yourself, or a significant other, that is greater than the way things are right now?

Let's get better acquainted with these three amazing friends that can improve every area of your life. Faith, Hope and Love were intended by God to be your intimate companions. They have the power to recode the DNA of your character. They bankroll character traits like peace, which comes from Faith; joy, which emanates from Hope; and compassion, which flows from Love. They bring you into alignment with the way God designed life to work.

Faith, Hope and Love are the three primary, positive, motivational forces in this world. They are powerful gifts from God. They give us the power to "not be overcome by evil, but overcome evil with good" (Romans 12:21). This is a big deal. The world is filled with evil that continually affects everyone's quality of life. The ability to overcome evil is a game changer. Faith, Hope and Love have the power to transform ordinary people into a force of righteousness. God intends to make you a light of his presence. If you are to accomplish your destiny, there is much to learn.

VIRTUE POWER

Faith, Hope and Love generate a resolute force of character. When Paul talked about "overcoming evil," he was not offering a cheap, trite religious slogan. He was a man who suffered much evil at the hands of others. He had a lot of evil to overcome. He learned the secret of how to rise above it: "overcome evil *with* good." Good is stronger than evil. Faith overcomes fear. Hope overcomes despair. Love overcomes resentment.

> Faith that overcomes: Distrust is a byproduct of evil. It hands the steering wheel over to fear. It puts Faith in the backseat and locks God in the trunk. Faith trusts. In the worst of circumstances it smiles knowingly toward God. Job, who suffered the loss of about everything, showcased the unbreakable motivational power of Faith. "Though He slay me, yet will I trust Him" (Job 13:15 NKJV). Faith conquers all fear.

> Hope that overcomes: A great many things can get us down. Paul "under fire" is a classic example of virtue on steroids. He pos-

sessed the disposition of a bulldog. Feel the motivational force of God's goodness emanating from his life! "I can do all things through Him who strengthens me" (Philippians 4:13). Hope triumphs over pessimism.

Love that overcomes: Hatred ignites a fire. The moment you try to fight evil with evil, you have lost. Jesus taught a better way than "an eye for an eye" (Matthew 5:38). "Love your enemies" (Matthew 5:44) is not a lofty aspiration. It is a natural way of life for people who are under the motivational power of Love. Love shatters vengeance.

GOODNESS ON DISPLAY

Christians do not have a good track record when it comes to showcasing virtue. Two unfortunate realities often unfold from a brief stroll through church history.

Christians displaying evil. Part of the sad history of the church is the frequent evil behavior of Christians. These are tragic examples of the Motivational Virtues being neglected and motivational evils springing up in their place. We'll explore the dynamic interplay of these conflicting motivations in later chapters.

Christians hiding from evil. Religion tries to distance itself from an evil world. Multitudes of the devout shunned the world and flocked to monasteries in the Middle Ages. The attitude still exists. I recall church admonitions in my youth: "Don't go to movie houses." Evil was like a virus—if you were not careful you might catch it.

The conquering way is not the cloistered way. What happens when virtuous people retreat from an evil world? Evil prevails. Jesus knows our context. His prayer in John 17:15 exposes his priorities: "I do not ask You to take them out of the world, but to keep them from the evil one." Jesus expects us to be engaged in this evil world to the extent that we need his prayers for protection.

The conquering way follows the way of Christ. He took evil head-on and won. You had better do some serious soul prep if you want to walk this way. When you are rightly motivated, evil is no match for you. Every form of darkness flees before the pure hot light of Faith, Hope and Love.

Paul, like every true disciple, was a man caught between two worlds. Listen to his short lament, as paraphrased in *The Message* version of the Bible: "Compared to what's coming, living conditions around here seem like a stopover in an unfurnished shack, and we're tired of it!" (2 Corinthians 5:3). Don't mistake his honest disclosure for any lack of resolve to be a force of goodness in the present world. "You won't see us drooping our heads or dragging our feet! Cramped conditions here don't get us down. They only remind us of the spacious living conditions ahead" (2 Corinthians 5:6 *The Message*).

Paul firmly hoped in the future but chose to live in the "now." His poignant visions of the afterlife were always balanced by a keen awareness of the present. "For *now* we see in a mirror dimly, *but then* face to face; *now* I know in part, *but then* I will know fully" (1 Corinthians 13:12). Paul had the maturity of perspective to equally grasp the present and the future. He interrupted his wondrous description of post-death life with two words: *But now* (1 Corinthians 13:13). They serve as a wakeup call. What should we focus on *now*? His answer is surprisingly simple: "*But now* faith, hope, love abide." Heaven will wait. Paul asserts that now is the time for the Motivational Virtues to shine in a dark world.

CHARACTERISTICS OF THE MOTIVATIONAL VIRTUES

Most people think of Faith, Hope and Love as sweet poetic quotations used at weddings. Wrong! They are fires of the soul that define a person's character. They are not behaviors to be practiced, but conditions of the heart to be nurtured. God wants to fill us with Faith, Hope and Love. They are the source and the sense behind the noblest of our behaviors.

Figure 2.1 illustrates how their effects are described in the Bible. They are the only true antidotes to evil. They are essential to the spiritual life and central to our personal development. One wonders why Faith, Hope and Love don't receive a greater emphasis in wider circles today. Clearly, we need a renaissance of a Virtues-based understanding of character development.

SYMPTOMATIC VIRTUES CATEGORIZED UNDER MOTIVATIONAL VIRTUES			
REFERENCE	LOVE	FAITH	HOPE
Galatians 5:22-23 Fruit of the Spirit	Love Patience Kindness Self-control	Faithfulness Peace	Joy Goodness
2 Peter 1:5-7 Peter's Summary List of Virtues	Moral Excellence Self-control Kindness Love	Diligence Knowledge	Perseverance
1 Thessalonians 1:3	Labor *prompted* by love	Work *produced* by faith	Endurance *inspired* by hope
Colossians 1:4-5	Love for saints	Faith in Jesus	Hope for heaven

Figure 2.1

The church has placed a great deal of emphasis on Faith, Hope and Love. As we saw in chapter one, many of the early church fathers considered them the "Cardinal [Primary] Virtues" of the spiritual life. Aquinas, considered one of the great theologians of the thirteenth century, wrote, "The whole perfection of this present life consists in faith, hope and charity."[1] Augustine, in the fourth century, claimed, "These are the three virtues . . . by which God is worshipped."[2] The apostle Paul, as we've seen, clearly understood and emphasized their central position.

What is so meaningful and unique about the Motivational Virtues? Why have they been so valued throughout church history? They stand alone in their power to transform the human heart. Faith-filled, Hope-filled and Love-filled hearts naturally and effortlessly produce an unending stream of goodness.

You may question, "Aren't there other virtues in the world?" Absolutely! But upon close examination, you will see that Faith, Hope and Love are uniquely able to motivate the heart. Temperance, for example, was one of the Cardinal Virtues espoused by the early church fathers. While it is undeniably virtuous to practice moral restraint and self-control over one's appetites, temperance lacks the inspirational power of the Motivational Virtues. Temperance is a natural consequence of Faith's trust, Hope's endurance and Love's passion. Faith, Hope and Love are the three spiritual artesian wells from which flows a world of unstoppable goodness.

CAUSES AND SYMPTOMS

Let's consider Love as we begin our journey toward understanding the Motivational Virtues. A Love-filled heart will, by force of nature, produce distinct and noticeable behaviors. Love is too powerful of a motivational force to remain hidden or unexpressed for very long. It is the goodness of God under pressure. If you have a heart condition of "Love" you will not have to convince anyone; you will manifest enough symptoms to prove it to yourself and to everyone around you.

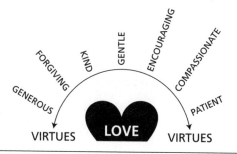

Figure 2.2

It is very important to distinguish between Love behaviors and Love itself. The Bible teaches that kindness and patience are manifestations of Love. "Love is patient, love is kind" (1 Corinthians 13:4).

Kindness and patience are not to be confused with Love. They are the *symptoms* of a Love-filled heart. They are what could be called "Symptomatic Virtues." They are virtues in that they are good, but they are symptoms because their motivational source is found elsewhere. They originate from Love.

Goodness "on display" inspires us and exposes our shortcomings. This is where many get lost on the path of self-improvement. It is easy to latch onto the admirable traits we see in others. Aspiring to be more kind makes sense and is even laudable. The problem is that symptoms, like kindness, lack the motivational power to change our lives. The pursuit of kindness, in and of itself, is an underpowered enterprise. Becoming a kinder person is not something we can accomplish directly. We need to shift our attention off the symptom and onto the motivational power that can help us achieve our desired objective. If we wish to be more kind-natured then we will have to grow in Love.

No one can consistently produce Love-like behaviors when their heart is not filled with Love. Behaviors need a power source. Consistently good behaviors depend on the existence of a "behavioral supply chain," which we discussed in the previous chapter. Good behaviors are the smoke that billows out of the fires of Faith, Hope and Love.

This brings us back to some fundamental truths:

- All behaviors are merely *symptoms*.

- Symptoms reveal the inward condition of our hearts.

- There is *always* a reason for the way that we act.

- We cannot manufacture goodness on demand.

- Goodness requires that we expand our hearts with the motivational power of Faith, Hope and Love.

In the chapters ahead, we explore the many cause-and-effect relationships between the Motivational Virtues and their associated symptoms. Most people are oblivious to the fact that there is a well-defined structure to the invisible, moral universe. Kindness, as we have seen, does not exist in isolation. It occupies a specific place within the larger framework of Love. The potential for sustainable personal growth is unlocked when we begin to understand the structured rationale behind why we do what we do.

DEFINING LOVE

Let's take a look at more symptoms associated with Love. "Love is patient, love is kind and is not jealous; love does not brag and is not arrogant, does not act unbecomingly; it does not seek its own, is not provoked, does not take into account a wrong suffered" (1 Corinthians 13:4-5).

DEFINING THE PRIMARY VIRTUE OF LOVE	
Defined by Symptomatic Virtues	**Defined by Symptomatic Evils**
Patient	Not envious
Kind	Not boastful
Rejoices with the truth	Not arrogant
Always protects	Not rude
Always trusts	Not self-seeking
Always hopes	Not easily angered
Always perseveres	Keeps no record of wrongs
	Does not delight in evil
	Never fails

Figure 2.3

Figure 2.3 outlines these verses from 1 Corinthians. It's interesting that Love is described more by what it is *not* than by what it *is*. There are three likely reasons for this:

1. Unloving people are more plentiful.

2. Unloving behaviors are more common.

3. Unloving people are conduits for evil.

What practical benefits can we gain from understanding the traits of those who are unloving? How can we best deal with unloving evil that is personally delivered to us?

- Recognize the symptoms.

- Understand the motivation.

- Realize that the problem is a character issue in the life of the offender.

We need to discern the root of evil if we are to overcome evil.

Each description of Love, whether positive or negative, provides important information on why people do what they do. When we understand our self and others it increases our people skills. This makes our life much easier. Below are some of the great benefits that come from seeing people as they are.

Reduced frustration: Once I understand someone's motivations I am far less likely to put unrealistic expectations on him or her. It would be pointless to expect much kindness from someone who has very little Love.

Insulation from evil: Motivational insights help us to deal with difficult people. We don't take their hurtful behaviors as just a personal affront. We are able to isolate the incident. We realize, "It's not my fault. It's their problem." Behavioral problems always stem from an internal character issue.

Better friendships: I am a better friend when I possess elevated insights into why people do what they do. I can more easily move beyond hurt feelings. I know that bad actions are always the results of motivational malaise. I know how to pray with insight for the offender. When opportunities arise, I am enlightened enough to speak into their life in a truly meaningful way.

More peace: Disturbers of the peace come knocking at the worst of times. It calms my soul when I grasp the big picture. Instead of becoming defensive or angry, I can train my soul to pause and ask, "Why are they doing that?"

More wisdom: When I understand the cause-effect relationship between motivations and actions, it increases my ability to understand a broad range of issues. If someone has an obsessive jealousy problem, I know that they have a significant Love problem. Love "is *not* jealous." I can work proactively with their root problem instead of giving them anti-jealousy advice.

Power over evil: Vindictive people practice full-contact evil. They are loveless. We know they are deprived because Love "does *not* take into account a wrong suffered." Understanding their motivational condition empowers me. I can rise above the actions and tongue-lashings of an enraged tormentor. I see a pathetic soul trapped in a Loveless existence. Compassion is not far behind. Love wins.

PEOPLE OF INSIGHT

It would be impossible to overstate the impacts that Faith, Hope and Love have on all our relationships. This includes the one we have with our self. God wants to make us *soul seers*. He wants us to know the heart condition of our spouse, children, significant others and everyone that he has placed in our lives. Only then will we be a qualified force of goodness to participate in being a part of the solution and not a part of the problem. If we are to achieve great relational skill as emissaries of God's goodness, we will need to gain a thorough understanding of the interplay between motivations and behaviors.

SEVEN UNIQUE EFFECTS OF FAITH, HOPE AND LOVE

Faith, Hope and Love are treated in the Bible in ways that no other virtues are treated. There is a wide body of biblical evidence that points to their unique roles in the spiritual life. We'll explore some of their distinctive roles below.

Seven Unique Impacts of Faith, Hope and Love
1. They _motivate_ every aspect of life.

Figure 2.4

Faith, Hope and Love motivate every aspect of life. Faith, Hope and Love are unique and distinctive among all virtues in that they have incredible power to motivate us. Let's examine their motivational merits in 1 Thessalonians 1:3: "We remember before our God and Father your work produced by *faith*, your labor prompted by *love*, and your endurance inspired by *hope* in our Lord Jesus Christ" (NIV).

There are three motivationally charged words that leap out from this verse: *produced, prompted* and *inspired.* They each address different elements that are essential to our personal development. We need all the production, prompting and inspiration we can get!

There are times when we need to bloom where we are planted and start *producing.* Then there are times when we need compassion to *prompt* us into action. Finally, there are seasons when we need to be reenergized by fresh *inspiration.*

Faith produces, Love prompts and Hope inspires. Together the Motivational Virtues have the power to deliver us from the doldrums of a mediocre life. The fact that they are *motivational* means they are designed to upset the status quo in your life.

Motivation is not just a good feeling. It is all about *action.* It involves more than a change in the way we think or how we perceive reality. Motivation actually produces something that is tangible.

Sometimes it is helpful to gain a deeper sense of a word's meaning by examining the various nuances of the original Greek words that were used.

Faith produces "work." The Greek word for "work" "denotes action or active zeal in contrast to idleness."[3] Faith produces an *active* spiritual lifestyle.

Love prompts "labor." "In secular Greek the word used here means 'weariness as though one has been beaten.' . . . Paul uses the same word to show that his work for Christ is a severe and exhausting burden."[4] Love prompts people to go the extra mile even when they feel completely spent.

Hope inspires "endurance." Paul used the same Greek word for endurance to describe his spiritual life, "steadfast endurance of sufferings."[5] Hope inspires people to never give up, due to their confidence in a greater tomorrow.

Motivation is a compelling reason why Faith, Love and Hope are so necessary to our lives. We all know how much we are in need of positive motivation. Think about the kind of spiritual progress we will make if the Motivational Virtues are prompting, producing and inspiring us to keep on working, laboring and enduring with a positive attitude!

The Motivational Virtues stimulate us to make an actual difference in the world. They work together to supercharge our personal lives. As we will see in our next point, each contributes in a different way to the development of our character.

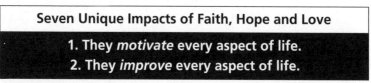

Seven Unique Impacts of Faith, Hope and Love

1. They *motivate* every aspect of life.
2. They *improve* every aspect of life.

Figure 2.5

Faith, Hope and Love improve every aspect of life. Faith, Hope and Love help develop specific areas of our character. We see this in these words of the apostle Paul: "We heard of your *faith* in Christ Jesus and the *love* which you have for all the saints; because of the *hope* laid up for you in heaven" (Colossians 1:4-5).

Each of the Motivational Virtues adds a specific component to our

Figure 2.6

personal development. Faith is about the quality of our inner spiritual connection. Hope is about the quality of our heavenly vision. Love is all about the quality of our relationships. One might call them the *inner, upward* and *outward* focal points for character development.

Faith: focuses us *inward* to the condition of our hearts. Are we worried or fearful? Faith is not just a belief in God's greatness; it is a deeply personal connection that engenders trust in God's complete goodness. It is not wishful thinking but truthful thinking. God is *all* good.

Hope: directs us *upward* to heavenly realities. It sees the circumstances of today in a much larger context. It grants an unshakable sense of purpose and destiny even in the worst of times. Hope makes us, in the words of Gordon Fee, "a thoroughly future oriented people."[6]

Love: points us *outward* to people. It motivates us to engage with others and their needs. The word *saint*, used in Colossians 1:4, is not reserved for a select few but is used in the Bible to describe an ordinary fellow traveler. Love targets relationships.

My life will certainly be improved if I have better relationships, inner confidence and operate with a profound sense of purpose. Who would want to surrender any of these far-reaching character traits?

It is important to remind ourselves that we do not live in a spiritually neutral environment. Evil constantly threatens to damage our relationships, erode our confidence and diminish our sense of purpose and destiny. Not to worry! Faith, Hope and Love have our backs covered in this area as well.

Seven Unique Impacts of Faith, Hope and Love

1. They *motivate* every aspect of life.
2. They *improve* every aspect of life.
3. They *protect* every aspect of life.

Figure 2.7

Faith, Hope and Love protect every aspect of life. Life can be deeply challenging. Circumstances can turn our lives upside down in a moment. Wild optimism can suddenly plunge into deep despair. Given the right circumstances, we are all vulnerable to many forms of evil. Frustration, anger, hurt, jealousy, bitterness, vengeance, lust, greed and many other things wait their moment to beckon for our attention. How can we guard our hearts from these dark intrusions?

The Motivational Virtues bestow much-needed and unique benefits in the most difficult of times. The Faith-filled, Hope-filled and Love-filled heart provides a natural antidote to evil. They do not make us impervious to wickedness, but they certainly diminish its effects and slow down its progression. They give us a grace zone to recover from troubled waters.

The Bible likens the Motivational Virtues to a suit of armor: "Let us be sober, having put on the breastplate of *faith* and *love*, and as a helmet, the *hope* of salvation" (1 Thessalonians 5:8). Due to the reality of ever-present evil, we are told to "put on" *this* armor. A breastplate is a portion of armor that is designed to protect the heart. A helmet protects the head. Together they guard our greatest vulnerabilities to evil.

Love protects the *heart* from hatred.

Faith protects the *soul* from fear.

Hope protects the *mind* from despair.

We need this kind of spiritual protection to worship God in an unfettered way. Jesus extolled this superior level of spiritual freedom: "You shall love the Lord your God with all your *heart*, and with all your *soul*, and with all your *mind*" (Matthew 22:37).

Seven Unique Impacts of Faith, Hope and Love
1. They *motivate* every aspect of life. 2. They *improve* every aspect of life. 3. They *protect* every aspect of life. 4. They *fulfill* every aspect of life.

Figure 2.8

Faith, Hope and Love fulfill every aspect of life. Some things are considered indispensable to having a good quality of life. The things most commonly put on this list are primarily material in nature. We all know that food and shelter are a part of our basic needs. It may surprise you to discover that Faith, Hope and Love are on the Bible's "must-have" list. Look at the extreme language that the Bible uses regarding our need to possess the Motivational Virtues:

Love: "If I . . . do not have love, I am nothing" (1 Corinthians 13:2).

Faith: "And without faith it is impossible to please Him" (Hebrews 11:6).

Hope: "If only for this life we have hope . . . we are of all people most to be pitied" (1 Corinthians 15:19 NIV).

It is obvious that there are absolute principles at work here. Faith, Hope and Love are not merely "nice-to-have" attributes. The words *nothing, impossible* and *pitied* make their absence a very dark day in the life of any soul that does not have them. Who wants to live in that realm?

Faith, Hope and Love are key priorities for leading a fulfilling life. Why is it that so many people do not have the Motivational Virtues at the top of their must-have list? How can these Virtues be so easily and widely ignored? The Virtues must be restored to their rightful place in the arena of personal growth.

These strong must-have statements about the Motivational Virtues make them chief among all virtues. The same claim is made no-where in the Bible regarding any other virtue. They are clearly unique and indispensable to a well-lived life.

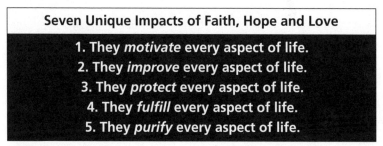

Seven Unique Impacts of Faith, Hope and Love

1. They *motivate* every aspect of life.
2. They *improve* every aspect of life.
3. They *protect* every aspect of life.
4. They *fulfill* every aspect of life.
5. They *purify* every aspect of life.

Figure 2.9

Faith, Hope and Love purify every aspect of life. God is actively involved in keeping and making our souls honest. Our capacity for self-deception makes this a necessity. When we are "true" on the inside, we have the capacity to be a positive light to those around us. Pretending never helped anyone.

It is important to realize that Faith, Hope and Love can be perverted into cleverly concealed counterfeits. More will be written about this later. There are times, for example, when Love may look like the real thing to us and to others but it is far from genuine. What appears to be Love is often just a cleverly concealed form of selfishness.

Beware of counterfeits! The Motivational Virtues need to be pu-rified on an ongoing basis for a good reason—Love can become lust; Faith can become presumption; Hope can become self-aggrandizement.

It is sobering to realize that these kinds of dark shifts can happen without an individual realizing it.

This is yet another aspect of the Motivational Virtues that makes them distinct and unique. Virtuous behaviors, like kindness and patience, do not require purification. Their purity is entirely dependent on the purity of the motivational condition from which they originate. If the Love is pure, then the kindness that flows out of it will be pure. Impure kindness is the result of an impure Love that spawned it. Impure Love takes on many deceptive forms. How many of us have received "kind" gifts only to later discover that there were expectations that came with them?

Streams must be purified at their source. The purity of Faith, Hope and Love determine the virtuous purity of our character traits and, ultimately, our behaviors. Look at how the Bible views this matter of purification.

> Faith: "The proof of your *faith*, being more precious than gold which is perishable, even though *tested by fire*, may be found to result in praise and glory and honor at the revelation of Jesus Christ" (1 Peter 1:7).

> Hope: "And everyone who has this *hope* fixed on Him *purifies himself*, just as He is pure" (1 John 3:3).

> Love: "Since you have in obedience to the truth *purified your souls* for a sincere *love* of the brethren, fervently love one another from the heart" (1 Peter 1:22).

Faith, Hope and Love are the three purification zones in our lives. They are the personal growth areas of our lives, and you can be assured that they have God's purifying attention. We do well to pay careful attention to them as well. Who would argue that the motivational streams of their soul do not require ongoing purification? Who wants to pretend they are something when they are not? Who would willingly live a life of self-righteous deception? If someone is unkind or disingenuously kind, they have a Love problem. They need to tend to their Motivational Virtues.

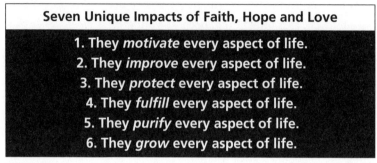

Seven Unique Impacts of Faith, Hope and Love

1. They *motivate* every aspect of life.
2. They *improve* every aspect of life.
3. They *protect* every aspect of life.
4. They *fulfill* every aspect of life.
5. They *purify* every aspect of life.
6. They *grow* every aspect of life.

Figure 2.10

Faith, Hope and Love grow every aspect of life. The Motivational Virtues expand the soul. Their expansiveness makes it impossible to contain them within the traditional religious confines of dos and don'ts. They transform our smallness of character into a demonstration of the largesse of God's character. One of the greatest things about life is that we are never stuck in our present reality. God has designed us to grow as human beings. The good news is that it is never too late to start.

King David poignantly wrote about God's ability to expand his soul: "You enlarge my steps under me, And my feet have not slipped" (Psalm 18:36). What began as a bold teenage warrior, facing Goliath's wrath, grew into the confident, long stride of a man who utterly trusted in God's enabling power. His increased capacity was a cause for praise to God. David described his personal growth when he wrote, "For by You I can run upon a troop; And by my God I can leap over a wall" (Psalm 18:29). God expanded his Faith to the point where he could fearlessly overrun an elite forces division of an ancient Amalekite army. That's growth!

So what does the nation-building, warriors-required, Israelite world of King David have to do with my life today? Simply this: God promotes our growth when and where we need it, given our situation.

What does personal growth look like for me? Two verses highlight the areas where God is actively working to expand us today.

Love and Faith: "We ought always to give thanks to God for you, brethren, as is only fitting, because your *faith is greatly enlarged*, and the *love* of each one of you toward one another *grows ever greater*" (2 Thessalonians 1:3).

Hope: "That you will *abound in hope* by the power of the Holy Spirit" (Romans 15:13).

Faith, Hope and Love are the motivational growth zones in our lives. These are the defined areas where the Holy Spirit is working to grow us "ever greater." When we ignore them as our personal priority for growth we cut ourselves off from our greatest potential as human beings.

The Motivational Virtues are at work in the enlargement of our character—additional evidence that they serve a very special and critical role. Paul, in the verses above, looked for, encouraged and praised noticeable increases in Faith, Hope and Love in the lives of those he mentored. We would no doubt be wise to do the same today.

Seven Unique Impacts of Faith, Hope and Love
1. They *motivate* every aspect of life.
2. They *improve* every aspect of life.
3. They *protect* every aspect of life.
4. They *fulfill* every aspect of life.
5. They *purify* every aspect of life.
6. They *grow* every aspect of life.
7. They *stabilize* every aspect of life.

Figure 2.11

Faith, Hope and Love stabilize every aspect of life. We live in such a busy world that we are constantly required to reshuffle and reorder our priorities. There are many things that clamor for the top spots on my calendar. These things constantly change. We are forced to ask, "What is the most important thing I have to do today?"

If I am washed overboard at sea, my priorities become greatly narrowed. "Keep swimming! Keep your head above water! Cry for help! Look for a lifeline or anything that floats!" What are my top priorities when it comes to navigating the treacherous currents of this life? What does the Bible say are my chief concerns? By now it should not surprise you to know that we are commanded to grab on to Faith, Hope and Love like our life depends upon it, and never let go. The Motivational Virtues are the key priorities of the spiritual life.

> Love: Red-Hot Passion—"Above all, keep fervent in your love for one another" (1 Peter 4:8).

> Faith: Dug In and Unmovable—"Continue in the faith firmly established and steadfast, and not moved away from the hope of the gospel" (Colossians 1:23).

> Hope: Grasping the Anchor—"Let us hold fast the confession of our hope without wavering" (Hebrews 10:23).

Notice the imperative and urgent language associated with Faith, Hope and Love in these verses. Phrases like *above all, firmly established* and *hold fast* make the point. These are inarguably the top priorities for personal growth.

FINAL THOUGHTS

Remember the words of Paul, "Your work *produced* by faith, your labor *prompted* by love, and your endurance *inspired* by hope in our Lord Jesus Christ" (1Thessalonians 1:3 NIV). Faith, Hope and Love are the secrets to living a life that *produces, prompts* and *inspires* positive forward movement!

Are there other things I could focus on? Perhaps. But the way I figure it, I am going to do pretty well if these three motivational forces are turned loose in my life. I want my Faith to be real enough so that

I naturally *produce* a steady stream of good works. I desire an inner tide of Love that *prompts* me to quickly respond when I might otherwise be too preoccupied to notice the needs of those around me. I want to be so filled with Hope in my eternal future that I am *inspired* with an unflagging endurance in the difficult circumstances I face today. If I am to live the motivated life that God has for me, the path forward will require an abundance of Faith, Hope and Love.

THE THREE GREAT ISMS THAT RULE THE WORLD

The Forces of Negative Motivation

> *Three sparks—pride, envy, and avarice—*
> *have been kindled in all hearts.*
>
> Dante, *Inferno* (VI, 74)

> *For all that is in the world, the lust of the flesh*
> *and the lust of the eyes and the boastful pride of life,*
> *is not from the Father, but is from the world.*
>
> 1 John 2:16

You may not know it yet, but you have a favorite "ism." The truth gets even uglier: you have had a long relationship with more than one ism. They have influenced your heart, your thoughts, and caused you to make some of the worst choices of your life. Who are these dastardly isms?

THE AGE OF REASON

The Enlightenment, also called the Age of Reason, which occurred in the 1600s and 1700s, gave rise to three modern philosophical terms:

egotism, hedonism and *materialism*. These were identified as three common motivational lifestyles. Look over the following descriptions and see which one you most closely identify with.

> Egotism: The pursuit of self-interest. "The drive to maintain and enhance favorable views of one's self that generally features an inflated opinion of one's personal features and importance—intellectual, physical, social and otherwise."[1]

> Hedonism: "The pursuit of or devotion to pleasure, especially to the pleasures of the senses."[2] It buys into the idea that it is morally and ethically right to do what is needed to achieve personal pleasure.

> Materialism: The pursuit of material things. "A preoccupation with material objects, comforts, and considerations, with a disinterest in or rejection of spiritual, intellectual, or cultural values."[3]

In spite of their modern-sounding names, the isms have been around for a very long time. They are three ancient, evil, motivational forces. The apostle John, in his first letter, wrote about them using their much older names. Before we name them let's look at the important way he introduced them: "For all that is in the world" (1 John 2:16). This far-reaching language used by John to set up the three primary evils is reminiscent of the inclusive way Paul described the Motivational Virtues— "But now faith, hope, love, abide these three" (1 Corinthians 13:13).

As we have seen, there is a large body of Scripture that identifies Faith, Hope and Love as the primary sources of all positive motivations. Get ready to enter a parallel universe! John introduces the subject of evil, giving us a new way of looking at humanity and understanding why people do what they do.

MOTIVATIONAL EVILS

John names the three ancient evils: "The *lust of the flesh* and the *lust of the eyes* and the boastful *pride of life*, is not from the Father, but is from the world" (1 John 2:16). These ancient lusts can be easily associated with the three isms.

EVIL AND ISMS	
Motivational Evils	**Modern Philosophy**
Lust of the Flesh	Hedonism
Lust of the Eyes	Materialism
Pride of Life	Egotism

Figure 3.1

The lust of the flesh, the lust of the eyes and the pride of life are not your ordinary, garden-variety evils. Like the Motivational Virtues, they are spiritual conditions of the heart. They each motivate a world of behaviors. These primary evils are the motivational forces behind every war, injustice, cruelty, murder, perversion, thievery, act of unkindness and despicable act of humanity throughout human history.

The "lust of the eyes," "the lust of the flesh" and "the pride of life" can be called Motivational Evils. What does that mean? It means that they are not just another typical evil behavior; they are spiritual forces of wickedness that captivate the heart and motivate or generate a world of evil behaviors. When you look at the emphasized words in the following Bible verses, it becomes clear that these three evils are motivational in nature and that they serve as the sources of all sorts of evil behaviors.

Lust of the Eyes / Materialism: "For the love of money is a root of all sorts of evil" (1 Timothy 6:10).
Application: A "root" is a hidden source that brings energy and life to its owner.

Lust of the Flesh / Hedonism: "Whose god is their appetite, and whose glory is in their shame, who set their minds on earthly things" (Philippians 3:19).

Application: There is no greater motivation than serving one's god.

Pride of Life / Egotism: "Do nothing from factional motives [through contentiousness, strife, selfishness, or for unworthy ends] or prompted by conceit and empty arrogance" (Philippians 2:3 Amplified Bible).

Application: The word prompted *is a highly motivational word.*

MOTIVATIONS AND SYMPTOMS

The Motivational Evils, like the Motivational Virtues, generate predictable symptoms. There is always a reason for the way we act. The three symptoms in figure 3.2, and their underlying motivations, illustrate the causal relationships behind why we do what we do.

THE BIBLE WITH MOTIVATIONS AND PHILOSOPHY		
Symptoms	Motivational Evils	Modern Term
Drunkenness	Lust of the Flesh	Hedonism
Workaholism	Lust of the Eyes	Materialism
Arrogance	Pride of Life	Egotism

Figure 3.2

The person who is armed with this knowledge of evil has a distinct advantage over the uninformed masses. It provides helpful insights into others' behaviors. It strengthens one's character in the heat of battle. The temptation to react to the evil actions of another lessens. The offender is understood in a much broader context. The recipient of evil comes to realize that there is an underlying root—a god or a prompting that drives them to do what they do.

The informed feel the trauma of the offender's dilemma more than the temporary impact of their evil actions and recognize that the offender is trapped in a web of evil motivations. People who respond in kind will not redeem the offender's character. The offenders are bound in evil. Where is the man or woman who has enough insight and love to positively engage them?

The knowledge of evil grants this kind of power. It improves one's people skills. It turns things upside down. The victim becomes the teacher. Darkness is eclipsed by light. God's love prevails over the hatred of man. Sin is stopped dead in its tracks. This is God's way. Good overcoming evil. Marriages restored. Friendships healed.

The knowledge of evil expands our souls. It makes us better spouses, parents, friends and mentors. Satan's flaming arrows are extinguished in the pool of godly insight.

EQ AND THE KNOWLEDGE OF EVIL

Having the knowledge of evil increases a person's "emotional intelligence (EI)." In 1990, psychologists Mayer and Salovey offered the first formulation of this concept. Until then, a person's IQ was used as the standard measurement for success in life. EI, or what is more commonly called EQ, has become universally accepted since then and is a significant metric for success in many fields, from education to business. Today, companies around the world often look through the EQ filter when hiring and developing their employees.

EQ had been defined as "our ability to handle ourselves and others. It is all about our ability to get along with others and build relationships."[4] It is now commonly understood that far more is required than having a high IQ to be successful in life. A high IQ can actually hinder a person's success. Nobody likes a know-it-all. This is especially true if they are out of touch with the effect that their displays of wondrous intelligence are having on the feelings of people around them.

Nothing helps to increase a person's emotional intelligence more than to understand the motivations of those around them. The Motivational Evils are deep currents that, like the Motivational Virtues, are often flowing at a subconscious level. They are more like feelings than calculated intelligence. A person does not wake up one day and say, "Today I am going to be materialistic! Let me see what I can acquire." Instead, they walk through a store, see something, and in the moment, "emotionally" want it. Emotions drive behaviors far more than intelligence.

Perhaps the most important gain from the knowledge of evil is personal. If we are to effectively manage our lives, we need a high EQ about our self. You may be deeply disappointed in yourself by something you said or did. The key to personal growth is to understand why you did it. Knowing why immensely helps you in your quest to overcome evil with good.

THE BLACK HOLE EFFECT

People become highly accustomed to lifestyles of hedonism, materialism or egotism. In many cases it's all they know. They get up every morning and are driven by their (often subconscious) emotional "needs." They want to feel good about themselves. Motivational fulfillment gives people a sense of well-being and purpose. They give little thought to what motivates them, yet their motivations define them.

The isms, or what the Bible calls the "lusts of this world," create two long-term problems for people:

Lusts are never satisfied. Evil always demands more and more at an ever-greater cost. Evil creates hungry souls who always lust for more pleasure, more possessions or more power. There is never enough. Evil offers no rest for a weary soul.

Lusts trap people in a gravitational field that crushes the life out of them. We start out choosing our lusts, and we end up serving them. They become cruel, unrelenting tyrants that twist our souls and rob us of our true purpose. Our lusts consume us like a black hole that threatens to suck everything into its influence until no light remains. Given enough time, these evils can become one's entire known universe.

God knows these truths about evil. Some people think that God is against evil because he does not want people to have fun. What utter nonsense! God knows how we are constructed and what truly satisfies the human spirit. God wants his children to live free from the tyranny of evil. He wants us to be filled with goodness and fulfilled in ways that we cannot even imagine.

But Satan has come to destroy. He wants to squeeze every last drop of happiness that he can from your life. Jesus said, "The thief comes only to steal and kill and destroy; I came that they may have life, and have it abundantly" (John 10:10). So with whom do you want to hang out?

A DEEPER LOOK AT THE THREE ISMS

Let's revisit the three isms and take a deeper look at their impact in people's lives.

Hedonism. Hedonism, as we will see later in the chapter, was the first of three great lies that Satan spoke to humankind. And it was alive and well almost two thousand years ago in the early church. The apostle Peter confronted this ancient evil motivation with some tough words: "For speaking out arrogant words of vanity they entice by fleshly desires, by sensuality, those who barely escape from the ones who live in error, promising them freedom while they themselves are slaves of corruption; for by what a man is overcome, by this he is enslaved" (2 Peter 2:18-19).

Hedonism elevates the pursuit of pleasure to ultimate importance.[5] This mindset is nothing new for those of us who live in the United States. We live in a culture beguiled by the promises of pleasure. This age-old lie captivates the minds of our youth and fills our university campuses with an *Animal House* party mindset. It enslaves people in every socioeconomic strata of society. The cost of this lust on a society is incalculable. Consider the following statistics.[6]

- Affairs affect 1 in 2.7 couples.

- 98% of married men and 80% of married women admit to fantasizing about someone other than their partner.[7]

- $13.3 billion was spent in the porn industry in 2006. US porn revenue exceeds the combined revenues of ABC, CBS and NBC.[8]

- Hotel viewership for adult films: 55%.[9]

- Adults admitting to Internet sexual addiction: 10%; 28% of those are women.[10]

- Over 15 million Americans are dependent on alcohol; 500,000 are between the ages of 9 and 12.

- Americans spend over $90 billion total on alcohol each year.

- The 2009 survey shows 25 million (one in ten) Americans surveyed reported driving under the influence of alcohol.

- Alcohol is involved in 50% of all driving fatalities.

- In the United States, someone is killed every 30 minutes in an alcohol-related traffic accident.

Hedonism, like all lusts, is never satisfied and always demands larger doses, more kinkiness and greater frequency. Sensuality of this kind displaces the rightful worship of God. It represents one of the worst exchange rates in human history. "For they exchanged the truth of God for a lie, and worshiped and served the creature rather than the Creator, who is blessed forever. Amen" (Romans 1:25).

You have to pity people who, at the end of their days, have lived all their lives in the pursuit of pleasure. Pleasure becomes ever more elusive as the body ages. When a person's health fails, they discover that the mere memory of pleasure is no pleasure at all. Bodily pleasures have forever escaped their grasp. What is left of life has no meaning. I shudder to imagine what the afterlife must be like for such shriveled-up, eternally hungry souls who, due to their dangerously unloving condition, have been permanently exiled from God and his community.

Contrast this with the immensely satisfied existence of those who have loved others and been generous to the needy. "But love your enemies, and do good, and lend, expecting nothing in return; and your reward will be great, and you will be sons of the Most High; for He Himself is kind to ungrateful and evil men" (Luke 6:35). Hedonism or Love? You'll need the right motivational power to walk in Love.

Materialism. Materialism sees "physical well-being and worldly possessions as constituting the greatest good and highest value in life."[11] It is the second great lie of the ages. It, too, has a very large and loyal following. While multitudes are primarily attracted and addicted to the wild pursuits of pleasure, many others are captivated by the allure of materialism.

In our consumer culture, advertisers constantly bombard us with all the things that we must have to be happy. Their messaging is spun a million different ways, but it boils down to one thing: If you possess what I am selling, it will increase your sense of personal significance. "Own this car and heads will turn in admiration as you drive by." "This housing development is for elite, special people like you." "Wearing these shoes or carrying this purse will cause others to have a higher regard for you."

The list of marketing pitches is endless. Their messages are not true. Materialism is one of the great spiritual lies of all time. The *International Herald Tribune* (the global edition of the *New York Times*) reports, "Using statistics and psychological tests, researchers are nailing down what clerics and philosophers have preached for millennia: Materialism is bad for the soul. Only, in the new formulation, materialism is bad for your emotional well-being."[12]

The article goes on to state, "In recent years, researchers have reported an ever-growing list of downsides to getting and spending—

damage to relationships and self-esteem, a heightened risk of depression and anxiety, less time for what the research indicates truly makes people happy, like family, friendship and engaging work."[13]

Rampant consumerism has come to the point worldwide where it creates a dilemma for the human race. The planet cannot continue to sustain our lust. "Today's consumption is undermining the environmental resource base." Researchers argue that consumerism needs to shift "priority from consumption for conspicuous display to meeting basic needs."[14] Good luck trying to get people to relinquish their god of materialism! Lusts are not only destroying individual lives; but they are also destroying the planet.

Jesus warned ages ago about the downsides of materialism. "Beware, and be on your guard against every form of greed; for not even when one has an abundance does his life consist of his possessions" (Luke 12:15). Jesus follows his warning with a compelling story of a rich man who was addicted to the accumulation of wealth. Like countless others in that situation, he determined to build bigger barns to hold all his possessions. The punch line of the story is the same one for everyone consumed by the spirit of materialism. "God said to him, 'You fool! This very night your soul is required of you; and now who will own what you have prepared?'" (Luke 12:20).

Materialism is one of the great, deceptive lusts of the world. Materialistic success comes at the immense cost of lost relationships and broken families. Countless and priceless opportunities to spend time with one's children and significant others are forever lost. The simple joys of life get trampled underfoot in the rush to constantly obtain more things.

Materialists, barring premature death, will spend their latter years planning either how to distribute all they've gained into the hands of others or how to die with it in their frail, firm grip. Materialism promises happiness, but at the end of life, it makes us beggars. Successful materialists, under the best of circumstances, will enter the next life as paupers. An unhealthy fixation on this world will leave a person ill prepared for the eternal one to come.

Don't forsake the advice of the greatest financial planner who ever lived. Try the Jesus plan! "Store up for yourselves treasures in heaven" (Matthew 6:20).

It is not uncommon, particularly among the young, to see the two extremes of hedonism and materialism coexisting side by side. Think of the party animal and the workaholic. The phrase "I work hard and I play hard" defines their mindset. It is often a fundamentally conflicted state of mind. What do I do now? Success demands work, and pleasure demands irresponsibility. They burn up their souls at an accelerated rate in the heated pursuit of consuming lusts.

Egotism. We now come to the third and final great lie of the ages. Egotism has been defined as "an exaggerated opinion of your own importance,"[15] and "an inflated feeling of pride in your superiority to others."[16] Perhaps you know someone like that!

Egotism is a tricky lust in a world that puts such immense value on talent, beauty and accomplishments. Accomplished people tend to have very high ego strength. Great accomplishments do not come easy. They require inner confidence, toughness and perseverance. This raises an honest question: Where do you draw the line between a good ego and an evil ego? Should people contentedly wallow in mediocrity and underachievement? Motivations are the key that unlocks this riddle.

Let's contrast the egotistical mindset with a great example of healthy ego strength. These words come from the pen of a man who has arguably done as much to influence Western history as anyone. The apostle Paul boasted, "I can do all things through Him who strengthens me" (Philippians 4:13). Paul exuded confidence to the max! It is the way he boasted that dramatically separates him from the lust of egotism. His bragging does not come from an egocentric, but from a God-centered, view of the universe. Paul shares with us his life principle:

"But he who boasts is to boast in the Lord" (2 Corinthians 10:17).

One writer offers four early warning signs of an overinflated ego and how it diminishes your chances for success. The principles are true in relationships and in the marketplace.

1. Being defensive: Defending ideas turns into being defensive.

2. Being comparative: Being too competitive actually makes you less competitive.

3. Seeking acceptance: Desiring respect and recognition interferes with success.

4. Showcasing brilliance: Ideas can be overshadowed by your own intelligence and talent.[17]

The same author goes on to share some good advice about things to watch out for in your struggle with your ego for personal significance.

1. Seeing someone you work with as a rival and thinking about how to "beat" them

2. Taking disagreement with your ideas personally

3. Compulsively following a competitor's "lead" so they're not doing anything you're not

4. Criticizing a competitor's strategies and prematurely discarding them as irrelevant

5. Believing you don't ever deserve to lose—a game, a conversation, a debate, a promotion, a raise, etc.—and you're not gracious in defeat

6. Disagreeing with someone's point just because they're the one who said it

7. Feeling worse about where you are when you see what others achieve[18]

It is important to remember that egotism is a lust that leads to temptation. In the heat of the moment, we can be tempted and overcome with the need to inappropriately advance our self. This sin, like all sins, diminishes us, the quality of our relationships and our opportunities in life.

How can we protect ourselves from the lust of egotism? It begins with an understanding that everything—every ability, every asset, every business opportunity—is a gift from God. Foundational to this is the knowledge at the core of our being that we are unworthy of God's goodness toward us. You know your heart is in the right place when an ego-strengthening experience of recognition genuinely humbles you and fills you with a heightened sense of worship and adoration for God.

TEMPTATION THROUGHOUT HISTORY

The original temptation. Now let's turn our clocks all the way back to the dawn of human history and figure out where all this evil came from. The Motivational Evils were the three tempta- tions that Adam and Eve succumbed to in the Garden. Those three represent the totality of all temptations. They were effective then, and they're just as effective now. "When the woman saw that the fruit of the tree was *good for food* and *pleasing to the eye*, and also desirable for *gaining wisdom*, she took some and ate it. She also gave some to her husband, who was with her, and he ate it" (Genesis 3:6 NIV).

THE ORIGINAL TEMPTATION		
Motivational Evils	**Modern Philosophy**	**Garden of Eden**
Lust of the Flesh	Hedonism	"good for food"
Lust of the Eyes	Materialism	"pleasing to the eye"
Pride of Life	Egotism	"gaining wisdom"

Figure 3.3

The three lusts that deceived the woman are illustrated in figure 3.3. The isms are Satan's strategic plan to bring us down and destroy us. Solomon said it ages ago, and it's still true today: "There is nothing new under the sun" (Ecclesiastes 1:9). What may appear to be temptations that are new and unique in our modern technological age are nothing more than repackaged versions of the original three isms.

The temptation of Christ. "And the tempter came and said to Him, 'If You are the Son of God, command that these stones become bread' . . . and said to Him, 'If You are the Son of God, throw Yourself down.' . . . Again, the devil took Him to a very high mountain and showed Him all the kingdoms of the world and their glory" (Matthew 4:3, 6, 8).

THE TEMPTATION OF CHRIST		
Motivational Evils	**Modern Philosophy**	**Wilderness Temptation**
Lust of the Flesh	Hedonism	"make these stones bread"
Lust of the Eyes	Materialism	"showed Him the kingdoms"
Pride of Life	Egotism	"throw yourself down"

Figure 3.4

The same three isms of deception can be seen in figure 3.4, when Jesus, who is called the second Adam in the Bible, was tempted. As context for this temptation, Jesus had just finished forty days of fasting and had become hungry when his temptations began. Satan used all the weapons of temptation in his arsenal. This time humankind, in Christ, overcame the three evil isms through the goodness of God.

The temptation of Solomon. The Bible records that Solomon was the wisest and richest man in his generation. He was the Bill Gates, Warren Buffett and Carlos Slim of his day. He possessed unlimited resources to pursue whatever he fancied. Over his long life, there were extended periods when he fell headlong into chasing the seductive motivations of all three of the great isms. His story is recorded in the first two chapters of the book of Ecclesiastes. It reveals the long-term, life-shaping power of the Motivational Evils to deceive even the wisest of souls.

THE TEMPTATION OF SOLOMON		
Motivational Evils	**Modern Philosophy**	**Garden of Eden**
Lust of the Flesh	Hedonism	"test you with pleasure" 2:1
Lust of the Eyes	Materialism	"all that my eyes desired" 2:10
Pride of Life	Egotism	"to know wisdom" 1:17

Figure 3.5

THE SYMPTOMS OF EVIL

The Motivational Evils generate evil behaviors or *symptoms* that are specific to each one of them, as illustrated in figures 3.6, 3.7 and 3.8, in which three lists of evil behaviors from the Bible are broken down according to their underlying motivations. As you look at the symptoms, perhaps you can start to identify how the isms are affecting your life and the lives of those closest to you.

"For men will be lovers of self, lovers of money, boastful, arrogant, revilers, disobedient to parents, ungrateful, unholy, unloving, irreconcilable, malicious gossips, without self-control, brutal, haters of good, treacherous, reckless, conceited, lovers of pleasure rather than lovers of God" (2 Timothy 3:2-4).

SYMPTOMATIC EVILS	AND ASSOCIATED		MOTIVATIONAL EVILS
REFERENCE	**LUST OF THE FLESH**	**LUST OF THE EYES**	**PRIDE OF LIFE**
2 Timothy 3:2-4	lovers of self unloving lovers of pleasure	lovers of money	boastful arrogant conceited

Figure 3.6

"Being filled with all unrighteousness, wickedness, greed, evil; full of envy, murder, strife, deceit, malice; they are gossips, slanderers, haters of God, insolent, arrogant, boastful, inventors of evil, disobedient to parents, without understanding, untrustworthy, unloving, unmerciful" (Romans 1:29-31).

SYMPTOMATIC EVILS	AND ASSOCIATED		MOTIVATIONAL EVILS
REFERENCE	LUST OF THE FLESH	LUST OF THE EYES	PRIDE OF LIFE
Rom 1:29-31	full of envy murder unloving unmerciful	greed	arrogant boastful

Figure 3.7

"For from within, out of the heart of men, proceed the evil thoughts, fornications, thefts, murders, adulteries, deeds of coveting and wickedness, as well as deceit, sensuality, envy, slander, pride and foolishness. All these evil things proceed from within and defile the man" (Mark 7:21-23).

SYMPTOMATIC EVILS	AND ASSOCIATED		MOTIVATIONAL EVILS
REFERENCE	LUST OF THE FLESH	LUST OF THE EYES	PRIDE OF LIFE
Mark 7:21-23	fornications murders adulteries sensuality	thefts coveting envy	pride foolishness

Figure 3.8

Jesus identified the location of the Motivational Evils with the phrase "for from within, out of the heart." James confirmed their point of origin: "What is the source of quarrels and conflicts among you? Is not the source your pleasures that wage war in your members?" (James 4:1).

We possess the nature of our forbears Adam and Eve. The Motivational Evils have germinated, found root and now grow within the soil of our fallen fleshly nature. That is why two of them are described in bodily terms, the lust of the flesh and the lust of the eyes. From Jesus to James, with many waypoints between, we come to understand the motivational makeup of the natural state of human nature. This is the ground where the isms rule.

FINAL THOUGHTS

Jesus conquered the three great isms and all their evil spawn. Satan's full-body temptation against Christ was futile. Jesus succeeded in the hot dry wilderness of a fallen world where Adam and Eve had miserably failed in a lush garden paradise. Paul writes, "'The first man Adam became a living being'; the last Adam [Christ], a life-giving spirit" (1 Corinthians 15:45 NIV). Jesus is humanity's great champion!

Jesus offers everyone who comes to him the same victory over the motivational forces of evil. This is the tantalizing way to change your character that Jesus spoke of when he exhorted, "Make the tree good and its fruit good" (Matthew 12:33). Paul elaborated on this foundational point for making spiritual progress: "Therefore if anyone is in Christ, he is a new creature; the old things passed away; behold, new things have come" (2 Corinthians 5:17). When Christ becomes an inseparable part of you through repentance and faith, there is a new kind of creature walking on planet earth. In Bible times the disbelieving public had a derisive term for them: *Christians*, which means little Christs.

The stage has now been set for a greater understanding of how to make spiritual progress. On the one hand, we have the Motivational Virtues, which are the supernatural product of the indwelling Spirit of God. On the other hand, we have the Motivational Evils, which are the natural product of our human nature. The two are at odds with one another. Spiritual progress requires spiritual conflict. In the next chapter we unfold a picture of the tricky ground we must learn to navigate.

4

THE BALANCES
OF MOTIVATION

Discovering Your Power Zone

> *Happiness is not a matter of intensity but of balance, order, rhythm and harmony.*
>
> Thomas Merton

> *Now to Him who is able to do far more abundantly beyond all that we ask or think, according to the power that works within us, to Him be the glory in the church and in Christ Jesus to all generations forever and ever. Amen.*
>
> Ephesians 3:20-21

Up to this point, the majority of our time has been spent establishing the essential value that Faith, Hope and Love bring to our lives. There is more to the story—they must be kept in balance.

Balance is something that we depend on every day. It keeps us on our feet. Without it we would be unable to walk. Balance requires energy and attentiveness. The stakes are exponentially raised when we get near the edge of a high bridge or building. Sometimes you can almost feel as if you are about to lose your balance and fall. Terrifying! Imagine walking a tightrope one thousand feet off the ground with no net. Who could relax? Balance requires a state of continuous vigilance. If I'm one thousand feet off the ground, maintaining my balance would vastly outweigh any other priority.

Keeping our character in balance is no less an important matter. Our character defines us. It has a profound effect on our quality of life and on those around us. It attracts people to us or repels them from us. It is the impression that comes to mind when people think about us. Lives have been ruined, marriages shattered, relationships destroyed, opportunities irreparably lost and careers obliterated due to character issues. Remarkably, most people are totally unaware of the dangerous character imbalances into which they can so easily slide and abide.

RELIGIOUS IMBALANCE

It is necessary to interject a cheerless fact at this point. Nowhere will you find more bizarre character imbalances than within certain religious circles. It is amazing how people can use "God" to cloak meanness, cruelty and bigotry. The roll call of the victims of religious abuse is a very long one. It is no wonder that so many are turned off by organized religion.

Before you get too hard on organized religion, consider another reality. Irreligious individuals make up a far greater percentage of malformed and unsafe personalities. The major difference is that nonreligious people usually don't tout moral superiority while acting dysfunctional.

Several years ago I had occasion to speak at a church near a large Amish enclave in Lancaster, Pennsylvania. After the speaking engagement, my hosts invited me to take a day trip into the Amish countryside. I had some free time and was eager to see for myself a society that had been largely frozen in time.

I had read about the particular Amish sect we would be visiting. They were a deeply religious people whose theology forbade them the use of modern technology. Their prohibitions were the result of a sincere and passionate desire to achieve moral excellence and purity. Their distinctive isolationist approach was due to a literal interpretation of the biblical concept of holiness—that is, to *separate* oneself from the world. Their exclusive use of horses for transportation, their simple dress and rules against electricity were all part of their deeply held religious belief system.

We headed out on a gorgeous, sunny spring morning, soon to get a far closer view of their world than I had anticipated. After we had driven for several miles into the countryside, I was struck by the lack of power lines and poles as far as the eye could see. It was like stepping back in time and viewing the earth as it was one hundred years ago. I lowered my power window to get a better look.

We turned up the drive of an Amish home with a sign advertising hardwood desks, and were directed to a large, unattached workshop at the side of the compound. The moment we entered, I was amazed by the quality of their handiwork. The cherry and black walnut roll-top desks were gorgeous and expensively priced. They might be behind on technology, but they were certainly up on current economics.

Then I noticed their tools. They had every cutting-edge pneumatic tool known to man, but their tools operated off of natural gas compressors. There were no electric power tools in sight. When I asked about their use of pneumatic technology, I was promptly informed that electricity was not good, but natural gas had been approved. Approved by whom, I wondered?

With my growing knowledge of applied Amish theology, we stopped next at a nearby house that was advertising homemade quilts. When I walked in the front door, I observed state-of–the-art propane lamps, propane stainless steel refrigerators and large freezers set within a very modern-looking kitchen. No electric plugs were in sight.

The Amish ladies were clad in homemade dresses fastened by straight pins (instead of buttons) that ran up the top half of the front of their dresses, with a solitary button at the neck. I learned that it had been decreed that one, but only one, button was allowed, and it had to be the top button. Button technology had been allowed one small intrusion. I asked myself if this was a revelation from God or if people just got tired of getting pricked in the neck.

It struck me that this was not a friendly religious environment for the uninitiated. To survive very long in these circles, you had better know the rules and know them well. The difference between acceptance and rejection could turn on one misplaced button. Like the Pharisees of old, they defined holiness with multitudinous ordinances that addressed many of the minutiae of life. I wondered how many rules there were.

We were looking over a stack of incredible, handmade quilts when one of my traveling buddies decided to cause trouble. He introduced me as a pastor to the group of Amish ladies in the room. I sensed their immediate and intense interest in me and felt a growing sense of discomfort. We had learned from them that they held church in their houses every week and traded off speaking responsibilities between them.

One outspoken woman with evenly placed straight pins marching down her chest promptly stepped inside my privacy bubble, looked me in the eye and asked me a very pointed question. I can still hear her distinctive melodic accent in my ears. "Do you use sermon notes when you speak?" The final word, *speak*, was drawn out as the highest note of the sentence. I somehow knew it was one of the *rules*.

The orange light from the propane lamps glistened off her straight pins, which started to look more and more like an ammo belt running down her torso. I paused. Her hard stare awaited my answer. I could see that the entire group of Amish ladies was poised and waiting while I formulated a response. Rejection was knocking at the door. I felt certain that this was similar to what Jesus must have encountered as the Pharisees surrounded him.

Part of me wanted to say, "God couldn't care less if you use notes or not!" Another part of me wanted to justify my position and declare, "God can anoint the preparation as much as the delivery." A mischievous side of me wanted to say, "I use a teleprompter from my computer-generated notes." Lacking a Jesus-quality answer, all I could eek out was a simple, "Uh yes."

Their collective body language in my peripheral vision told the story. The woman in front of me raised her bony nose to a practiced angle and intoned, "Ahhhhhhh, we *never* use notes." They were holy, and I was a reprobate pastor! They could speak directly from God. They were blessed. Silly me! My congregation only got secondhand notes. Yet I was honestly surprised at how deeply I felt the sting of their collective rejection.

It was a significant irony that I ended up purchasing a gorgeous wall hanging with a portion of 1 Corinthians 13 hand-stitched on it from the spokeswoman. My eye paused with some amusement over the final line, "the greatest of these is love." I headed out the door with my treasure in hand and an unforgettable lesson in holiness run amok.

My encounter with the Amish showed me how easy it is for well-intentioned people to become misdirected. They were faithful to the letter of the law *as they understood it*. But you can't make me a better person by passing more rules. This is the problem with a "religious" mindset. Religion focuses on the *things* I think I *should* do. It creates long lists of regulations.

Even if I just follow Bible laws, I am left holding a huge grab bag of things I *should* do. I already know how imperfect I am. I do not need to be told over and over again what I should do. I need help doing it!

THE ANTIDOTE TO IMBALANCE

The apostle Paul invalidated all legalistic approaches to personal growth. "[Christ] made us adequate . . . not of the letter but of the Spirit; for the letter kills, but the Spirit gives life" (2 Corinthians 3:6).

Laws and letters only prove just how far short of the mark I am. God's law is perfect; I am imperfect. But I do not need condemnation; I need acceptance.

I need a relationship with someone who will help me. This is the Spirit's mission. "The Spirit . . . will guide you into all the truth" (John 16:13). He is our guide. He will lift us to our greatest potential. He is the *power source* of the Motivational Virtues. Notice how clearly this is spelled out in the following three verses.

> Faith: "We through the Spirit, by *faith*, are waiting" (Galatians 5:5).

> Hope: "That you will abound in *hope* by the power of the Holy Spirit" (Romans 15:13).

> Love: "The *love* of God has been poured out within our hearts through the Holy Spirit" (Romans 5:5).

We cannot be all that we want to be, without the participation of the Spirit. His mission is to improve our character. This is a good place to revisit the primary role of the Spirit in one's behavioral supply chain that was introduced in chapter one.

---

5 FACTORS THAT DETERMINE OUR BEHAVIORS – FACTOR #5

Our Behaviors ← Our Character ← Our Motivations
Our Master ← Our **Heart** (IS LIBERATED BY) The **HOLY SPIRIT**

Figure 4.1

We also need to know that there is another character on the dance floor. Paul fills in the rest of the picture for us. "The sinful nature wants to do evil, which is just the opposite of what the Spirit wants. And the Spirit gives us desires that are the opposite of what the sinful nature desires. These two forces are constantly fighting each other, so you are not free to carry out your good intentions" (Galatians 5:17 NLT).

The Spirit is pulling us in the direction of Faith, Hope and Love. The flesh, as we learned in the previous chapter, is pulling us in the direction of the lust of the flesh, the lust of the eyes and the pride of life. So depending on the spiritual maturity of the individual, "The Holy Spirit" could be replaced with "The Flesh" in figure 4.1. The winner of these competing forces determines the makeup of our motivations, character and ultimately our behaviors.

A few verses later, Paul unpacks a key strategy for making spiritual progress within such a conflicted environment. "For the one who sows to his own flesh will from the flesh reap corruption, but the one who sows to the Spirit will from the Spirit reap eternal life" (Galatians 6:8). Sowing is about investing. All spiritual progress requires an investment.

Many years ago there was a television commercial that advertised a type of glue that was uncommonly powerful. To demonstrate its power, two wood blocks were glued together and hooked to chains that were attached to the back of two opposing trucks. The trucks spun their wheels in a cloud of dust and burning rubber trying to pull apart the bond of glue.

This television commercial is a lot like the battle between the Spirit and your flesh. How can we prevail in such a highly charged, stressful, competitive atmosphere? It comes back to sowing. Stop putting gas in the wrong truck! Invest in your spiritual life and you will ensure the eventual winner. We need to focus on life with the Spirit and ask how we can better cooperate with him.

There is more to the struggle. We need to more fully understand the nature of the tensions that exist between flesh and Spirit. This brings us to the subject of imbalance and the power zone.

MOTIVATIONAL IMBALANCE

Imbalance among the Motivational Virtues occurs in one of two ways. They can be diminished or they can be hyped up. The flesh leads to both imbalanced conditions.

Diminished Faith, Hope and Love require little explanation. Everyone deals with experiences that have the potential to reduce one's

Faith, Hope and Love. It takes force of character not to succumb to brooding evil in the face of scary, discouraging and hateful realities.

If Satan can't diminish your Faith, Hope or Love, he has one more option. He can try to hype them up. Each of these virtues can be overdone to the point where they become a deceptive parody of the real thing. Grand professions of Faith can mask self-promoting presumption. Positive proclamations of Hope can disguise a sense of self-aggrandizing entitlement. Passionate demonstrations of Love may camouflage self-serving manipulations. Hyped Faith, Hope and Love are suffocating forms of self-centeredness.

The Motivational Virtues reside in the balanced middle of the power zone where they are fueled by the prevailing presence of God's Spirit. True virtue is always a balance. This is nowhere more important than in the Motivational Virtues.

The power zone is where our character is most God-like. Some call this condition "godliness." This is the region where the character traits associated with the virtuous motivations of Faith, Hope and Love flourish and ultimately determine our behaviors. The power zone and the bidirectional imbalances of Faith, Hope and Love are illustrated in figure 4.2.

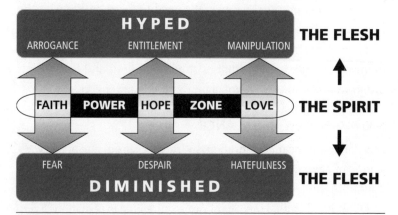

Figure 4.2

The more we move away from the power zone, the more our motivations become tainted by evil. *Diminished* virtues make us increasingly vulnerable to the negative forces of fear, despair and hate. *Hyped* virtues overdo a good thing and open the door to the dark deceptions of arrogance, entitlement and manipulation. Imbalance is the road that leads to increasingly dysfunctional personalities. The balance that occupies the middle between diminished and hyped virtue is a sweet spot for the soul. This is the Spirit-empowered precinct where the heart is freed from both negative forces and dark deceptions.

THREE RELIGIOUS EXTREMES

Most people know that diminished Faith, Hope and Love are not good things. A diminished condition will not help your image as a spiritual leader. *Hyped* Faith, Hope and Love can have the opposite effect. Religiously hyped people, to the uninformed, can look to be highly qualified spiritual leaders. But they are dangerous to themselves and to others. They need to be understood, exposed and set free by the truth.

Let's examine three classic religious character imbalances that are the result of people being *hyped* out of the power zone. It is a great irony that people with the following toxic imbalances think of themselves as great leaders and holy representatives of God. These distortions of Faith, Hope and Love are revisited in much greater detail in upcoming chapters.

The hyped-Faith persona: Holiness is a license for control of the universe. Hyper Faith deceptively shifts the focus off of trust and confidence in the faithfulness of God and onto one's personal merits. It is a path to unbridled pride. Hyper Faith says, "Look at *me!*" It is about how much faith *I* have. It places an undue and unbearable burden upon its bearer. It diminishes one's dependence and need of God. Who needs God when you have God's promises in your awesome believing hands? Boldness is the order of the day.

Hyper Faith is presumptive and tramples down appropriate boundaries in how it relates to God. Gone is the role of a humble supplicant before its King. In its place is an authoritative figure that talks to and at God. It should not be surprising that hyper Faith overruns healthy boundaries with people too. It feels divinely qualified to meddle, direct and control the lives of others. This hyped condition misses the connectedness and intimacy with the Creator that is at the heart of the power zone of Faith.

The hyped-Hope persona: Holiness is a license for privileged living. Hyper Hope deceptively shifts the focus off of the future and onto the present. It confuses our eventual glorious exaltation in Christ with our present humble state of affairs. It generates wishful thinking and misdirected hopes in this present world. Hyper Hope needs to understand that "our citizenship is in heaven, from which also we eagerly wait for a Savior, the Lord Jesus Christ; who will transform the body of our humble state into conformity with the body of His glory" (Philippians 3:20-21). Given our notorious past, such a mind-boggling Hope should humble, amaze and fill us with unending gratitude.

But instead, hyper Hope says, "Look at who *I* am! Look at what *I* am doing!" It makes one feel like part of a special, privileged class. It generates a totally inappropriate attitude of personal entitlement. Predictably, it casts a critical and condemning eye toward others of lesser stature. Egocentric service loses the joyful connection with God (who delights in our advancement), which is at the heart of the power zone of Hope.

The hyped-Love persona: Holiness is a license for using others. Hyper Love deceptively shifts the focus off of giving and onto taking. The hallmark of true Love is that it gives without expecting anything in return. Jesus personified this on the cross. Hyper Love is a sticky mess. Gifts are given, but obligations are attached. This kind of giving is nothing more than a thinly disguised form of manipulation.

Hyper Love is driven by unmet and unrelenting personal neediness. Unable to absorb the amazing, unconditional love of God, it grasps for personal esteem through the affirmations of others. Having bypassed perfect Love it finds no suitable substitute. Its unabated neediness is masked by emotive demonstrations of Love for God and others. Codependent relationships cannot backfill the bottomless void of lost intimacy with God. This hyped condition is disconnected from the overflowing unconditional love of God that is at the heart of the power zone of Love.

UNDERSTANDING AUTHENTIC SPIRITUALITY

Much of the confusion that gives rise to the imbalanced personas above has to do with a fundamental misunderstanding of the Bible word *holiness*, which is misunderstood almost as much by church-goers as it is by irreligious people. Should we be surprised?

"Holiness" sounds like stuck-up religious lingo. Its only colloquial use is the phrase "holier than thou."[1] "I am better than you!" is not a positive image for a word. Given this stigmatized usage, it is no wonder that the word has fallen on hard times. Christians sing it in worship, but few understand its true meaning.

Holiness is a Bible word with profound meaning. Without digging too deep, it means "being God-like in your character." It is having a heart filled with balanced Faith, Hope and Love. In short, it is living in the power zone.

People develop some very strange ideas about what it means to be holy. Some see it as a rigid adherence to restrictive religious rules, where disobedience brings the direst of consequences. They are too spooked to have much fun. No happy parades for you!

For those familiar with ancient Bible stories, holiness may conjure up bizarre images. I think of leather-skinned prophets of God sitting in the hot desert sun in itchy clothing, eating crunchy locusts with honey dip on the side. It's no wonder that believers can have a hard time relating to biblical holiness.

Who made the rule that you can't have a great time, be normal and be a highly spiritual person? Holiness, in the truest biblical sense, is a peaceful (Faith-filled), joyful (Hope-filled), loving (Love-filled) existence. It's not uptight. No straight pins for my shirt!

We need to understand that God's laws are not designed to ruin our fun. They are to protect us from our own destructive tendencies. Henry Blackaby reminds us, "The commands are for your own good."[2] When God commanded "Be holy," he was looking out for our happiest, healthiest interests. Living a holy life does not mean that you need to do extreme things like move to a monastery, quit going to movies or cease all forms of fun and entertainment. Dallas Willard reminds us that this kind of spiritual misdirection happens when "we don't approach and receive the life that Jesus offers in the right way."[3]

An authentically spiritual life frees us up on the inside so we can more fully enjoy God's blessings. The apostle Paul embraced enjoyment as an integral part of superior moral character: "God . . . richly supplies us with all things to enjoy" (1 Timothy 6:17). We have lost our balance in Hope when we lose the luster of prevailing joy.

JUDGING OTHERS

People understandably hold their religious belief systems very near and dear to their hearts. It is an irony that in their zeal to defend and promote the truth, as they see it, people often demonstrate highly unloving attitudes and unholy behaviors. They fail to distinguish between their commitment to the truth and the way they treat people. This is a high-speed rail ticket out of the power zone.

The Bible gives some very specific and tender instructions for those who are in a leadership position that requires them to pass judgment on others: "If anyone is caught in any trespass, you who are spiritual, restore such a one in a spirit of gentleness" (Galatians 6:1). Judgment is always for the purpose of, and in hopes of, restoration, never condemnation. This is representative of a sweet balance within the Motivational Virtue of Love.

Many religious leaders have not made a good showing in the judging department. On more than one occasion, so-called holy men of God exacted cruel and unusual punishments upon those they deemed unholy. The victims of the Spanish Inquisition and the Salem witch trials stand as an unforgettable testimony to just how badly holiness can be misconstrued.

While few of us today are in danger of being burned at the stake, we are very much at risk of incurring the self-righteous judgments of spiritually imbalanced people. The false spirit of judgmental "holiness" that generated so many abusive horrors of the past is still flourishing today. I can practically guarantee you that such a person lives within striking range of you. Some likely attend your church. See them for what they are and avoid their false, destructive distortions of holiness.

POWER ZONE OUTCOMES

The nearer we live to the center of the power zone, the more our nature succumbs to the influence of God's Spirit. We have discussed the agenda of the Spirit. His activity causes us to abound in the Motivational Virtues. Faith, Hope and Love are the three growing fields in which God has called us to flourish. They are the soils in which the advancement of our character will blossom or whither.

Picture yourself basking in the middle of a warm, sunny, Love-filled field with a good friend. It is a balmy, blissful day. What could possibly pull you out of the power zone? You are just starting to feel spiritually advanced when a hot, blistering wind shatters your paradise. Your judgmental "friend" speaks intentionally hurtful, untrue words. In a moment heaven becomes hell. Its withering heat feels insufferable. You are the recipient of a hateful act.

It is easy to stay in the power zone when you are surrounded by manifold blessings. But what about temptations? We need them! They test the strength and purity of our motivations.

In our example of shattered paradise, will Love or hatred win?

Long shoots of compassion that have been tenderly growing are at risk. Will they be burned back until only a blackened, smoking stump of resentment remains? Or will Love prevail and even grow in the face of such a tormenting tornado?

Welcome to a growth moment. Paul called these kinds of attacks "the flaming arrows of the evil one" (Ephesians 6:16). Emotions are enflamed. You are drowning in hurt and anger. You may find yourself transported to a troubled moment in your childhood. The enemy's arrow has struck a deep place that Love has not yet healed. Or you may be consciously unaware why the words have stung so deeply. Your old nature erupts in pain. The flesh begs for retaliation. The battle for your character is in full sway. Will you make a wounded retreat? Will you skillfully calculate how to disable the offender? Will you make a forceful counterstrike? Evil begets evil.

There is another path that requires insight. You can resist evil. You can pray. God is with you! You may sense the power of the Spirit lifting you above the power of evil. Freed from the grip of the flesh, things look different. You are able to take your eyes off your pain. You gawk at your offender. You see a hurting, diminished, pathetic soul. Compassion blossoms. Love wins. You have found power in the power zone.

SPIRITUAL TOPOGRAPHY

We always fight our character battles on well-established terrain. This is good news. There are no surprises. There is no new line of attack that will take us off-guard and surprise us. Had their been another angle of temptation, Satan would surely have used it against Jesus. The lust of the flesh, lust of the eyes and the pride of life continue their unabated, ancient appeals to the flesh. The Spirit faithfully causes the growth of Faith, Hope and Love to counter them. God wants us to rise above our fleshly origins and become spiritual creatures who reflect his glory on the earth. This is the brilliance of the power zone.

The battlefield of Love, described in the scenario above, is one of three battlefields. It has a recognizable topography. The same is true with the battlefields of Faith and Hope. In the midst of the battle we suddenly realize, "I have been here before. I've seen these landmarks." We need to train ourselves to discern the landscapes on which God has called us to grow. Is this a struggle for Faith, Hope or Love?

Satan has an intimate knowledge of the landscapes upon which he will confront us. "Your adversary, the devil, prowls around like a roaring lion, seeking someone to devour" (1 Peter 5:8). He took down Adam and Eve, and he is looking to defeat you. His attacks are always intended to diminish or hype our Faith, Hope and Love. To the extent that he can influence our motivations, he has won the battle.

So we need to keep our focus on the front lines. Ask, "Is this the main battle or am I fighting a secondary battle?" The circumstances right in front of us are rarely the main issue in a character battle. It is easy to be distracted by side issues like right and wrong, justice and injustice, or truth versus a lie. Our sensibilities have been offended, and we are ready to go to war. I have watched my children bicker over who said what and call each other liars, oblivious to the diminishment of their character. I have seen the same behavior between responsible, intelligent adults, myself included! Beware! These battles often deplete the emotional resources that are required to win at the front lines.

Fight these battles, if you must, but don't do so at the expense of your character. Dress up like a holy warrior and fight for truth and justice. Keep in mind that these battles are side skirmishes. Do what you believe God has called you to do. Just don't mistake your cause success for character success.

The real battle, the one that counts for the long haul, is the battle for your character. At the end of the day, after all the confrontation and jostling for truth are over, you need to ask yourself one question: "Is my heart more or less filled with Faith, Hope and Love?" If you have been diminished in virtue, the price for your foray was far too high. God's main agenda for you is always the advancement of your character. He has another plan to deal with injustices.

At SpiritualProgress.com you can take a free online character assessment and see where you plot in nine unique graphic views, including the character map. Invite friends and family or small group members to assess you. This is often the more accurate measurement. You can take the assessment multiple times and track your progress in Faith, Hope and Love.

The power zone, as we have learned, is the sweet, balanced spot between hype and diminishment. The character map (figure 4.3) provides a high level and comprehensive view of the character growth zones of Faith, Hope and Love. It illustrates how important it is to keep the Motivational Virtues in balance.

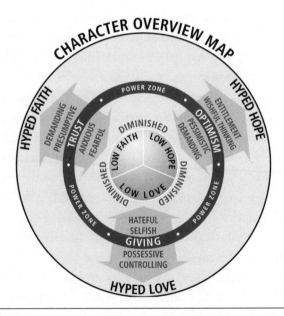

Figure 4.3

OVERCOMING DIMINISHMENT

Diminishment is always the result of too much self-sufficiency. The extent of our self-reliance determines how well we navigate the achievements and the disappointments of life. Paul knew the secret of how to maintain his motivational balance: "I know how to get along with humble means, and I also know how to live in prosperity; in any and every circumstance I have learned the secret of being filled and going hungry, both of having abundance and suffering need" (Philippians 4:12). What was Paul's secret? It boils down to two questions.

1. Will worldly success lull me into a false sense of pride and independence? Do I imagine myself to be self-made? Distancing oneself from dependence on the Spirit is the shortest path to the diminishment of Faith, Hope and Love. Paul gives a sober warning: "I say to everyone among you not to think more highly of himself than he ought to think" (Romans 12:3).

2. Will I choose to let pain and loss define my view of the world? Do setbacks and disappointments have anything to do with our inherent value as a person? We must learn to embrace our sufferings as a great friend and ally in the development of our character. This is the Bible way. "Consider it all joy . . . when you encounter various trials, knowing that the testing of your faith produces endurance. And let endurance have its perfect result, so that you may be perfect and complete, lacking in nothing" (James 1:2-4).

Faith, Hope and Love can be equally diminished by our successes and failures. Yet virtue can flourish in the midst of prosperity and poverty. No circumstance has the power to diminish our character without our permission.

OVERCOMING HYPE

The central issue of hype also has to do with a false sense of self-sufficiency. Are we foolish enough to imagine that we are the source rather than the recipient of all good things? Do we imagine that Faith, Hope and Love are somehow dependent upon us rather than the other way around? Do we think they are character traits that we can conjure up on demand?

The worst thing we can do is to put on the posture of Faith, Hope and Love when we do not possess their motivational power. The world doesn't buy it. They look at our composed piety in disgust. They see, all too clearly, the ugly realities of pessimism, selfishness and anger that bristle just beneath the surface of our "religious" skin. We need to reject the smiling face of self-righteousness and opt for humble honesty. Everyone can relate with someone who is struggling. No one likes a phony, even a sincere religious one.

Nonreligious people look at the veneer of Christian personas and mock the church. Hyped-up virtues are evil. They are pungent antidotes to the development of healthy character. They create toxic environments that hurt people. They are demonically inspired and deeply entrenched belief systems. Humble dependence on God is the truth that sets us free and keeps us in the power zone.

THE FORCES OF IMBALANCE

Faith

Diminishment: Faith must be fortified. Left unattended, the weeds of worry soon blossom into a tangled maze of insecurity. Troubles are unavoidable, but they are an opportunity to grow. When Faith is diminished we begin to feel that God is the culprit. His character becomes the focus instead of our character. "Why, God?" opens the door to diminished faith. Fear and anxiety move in and start decorating the house. True Faith says, "I do not understand but I trust in God's goodness!"

Hype: Faith can be hyped up into religious extremism. It looks like the genuine article but it is a cleverly concealed form of self-reliance. Dependence on God is replaced with presumption. Hyper-Faith people start to order God around. Reliance shifts from the presence and character of the Promiser to "their" interpretation of the promises. They need a deepened personal connection back to their watchful Creator who is committed to their highest good.

Hope

Diminishment: Everyone faces Hope-crushing moments. The loss of Hope is a slippery slope that can quickly lead to despair. I have heard the cry from the bottom of the hill: "I have nothing left to live for!" But our present afflictions are temporary, and they work in our favor. They create opportunities to build our character. Hope emboldens us to endure adversity. It is unstoppable. True Hope stands on the high ground of having an eternal perspective.

Hype: Hyper Hope lays bold claims to heaven but its treasures lie elsewhere. False motives drive the pursuit of temporal, worldly objectives. This misdirection is propagated through distorted "Christian" messages. "You are royalty! You will reign with Christ! You are entitled to the best! Earthly prosperity is your divine right." This false doctrine is nothing more than wishful thinking. No one has ever been helped by unrealistic expectations. True Hope knows, "I deserve nothing! But God has already given me everything that is important in this life and beyond."

Love

Diminishment: Love requires that we be vulnerable. It often ventures way out on a limb of compassion. This does not leave a person in a good defensible position. Hurtful words and actions can devastate the heart and set the stage for highly self-destructive exchanges. A quick bitter response exposes the shallowness of our Love. Resentment is a virulent poison of the soul. Forgiveness from the heart is the antidote that offers a 100 percent cure rate.

Hype: Emotional neediness is a lusty condition that desperately cries for fulfillment. It opens a wide door for mountains of bad decisions. This shallow life is typified by the pursuit of misguided relationships, fleeting friends and foolish investments that produce no returns. It develops codependent strategies to ensnare its victims. This desperate state of neediness can only be healed by God's unconditional Love.

FINAL THOUGHTS

You cannot achieve your potential without the motivational forces of Faith, Hope and Love. They need to be nurtured. They must be kept in balance to stay close to the center of your power zone.

Evil knocks at the door. The enlightened resident takes a quick glance and says, "I recognize this! I'm not going down that path!" Truth opens eyes and inoculates people from evil. Once you have seen the motivational landscapes upon which character is formed, you can never be the same.

The chapters ahead will fully expose the motivational forces associated with good and evil. Motivational change is the key to behavioral change. The Spirit changes our motivations. May you be transformed into God's goodness as the Spirit multiplies your Faith, Hope and Love!

5

MOTIVATIONAL EXERCISE
The Work of Character Development

> *Spiritual practice is simply a way for us to position ourselves so that Christ can dwell within us.*
>
> Richard Foster, *Life with God*

> *Exercise daily in God—*
> *no spiritual flabbiness, please!*
> *Workouts in the gymnasium are useful,*
> *but a disciplined life in God is far more so,*
> *making you fit both today and forever.*
> *You can count on this. Take it to heart.*
>
> 1 Timothy 4:7-9, *The Message*

As I drove toward the abbey, I struggled with deeply mixed emotions. The brilliant, green countryside of British Columbia was pierced by random outbursts of color from pink and purple wild rhododendrons. Sun breaks mottled the verdant hills with shadows that gave them a breathtakingly textured beauty. None of this managed to quell my growing misgivings.

I was headed for a spiritual retreat sponsored by Regent College. When I picked up the instruction packet earlier that day, I learned a couple of things that caught me off-guard. First, it was to be a silent retreat. *What*, I wondered, *is a silent retreat?* The term unsettled me. How can you learn anything if it's silent? I patted my laptop computer on the seat beside me with a sense of consolation.

Second, the location was a bit out of my comfort zone. I had never been to an abbey, and it seemed more than a bit weird to a Protestant pastor steeped in church growth principles. Attendance had been strictly limited to a small group of thirty; for better or worse, I was committed.

Dr. Eugene Peterson, a significant writer in the field of spirituality and author of *The Message*, was to be our personal spiritual docent. His presence as the guide had first convinced me to sign up. I hung on to the hope that Dr. Peterson's leadership would make the weekend worthwhile. I also did not want to face Dr. Peterson, my professor, back on campus after ditching his retreat.

I turned into the modest entrance of the abbey and navigated my car up the long driveway that intersected the meticulously manicured grounds. I was genuinely surprised by the sense of intimidation I felt as I pulled up to the complex of mission-styled buildings. It felt uncomfortably religious and a little bit spooky.

Fortunately, I soon found a familiar face from Regent, got directions and checked in. Then I headed to my room, a very small space with the narrowest bed I had ever seen and a lamp. That was it. At least the bed had a mattress. A communal restroom was down the hall. I dropped my bag on the tiny bed and headed out to unobtrusively explore the place before the start of our opening session.

We gathered in a simple room, with chairs set up in an elongated circle. I slid into one of the chairs and carefully eyed the group members as they entered and sat down. I could tell from the number of Birkenstock-clad feet that these were not the kind of folks I typically hung out with. The hushed tones told me that word had gotten out about this being a silent retreat. Dr. Peterson sat along the middle of one long side of the oval and started the meeting with a smile as total silence settled over the room. His opening words floored me and confirmed my worst fears. He calmly stated, "This weekend is purposeless."

Purposeless! What a worthless word! My mind began to spin with all of the important things I could be doing back home. While I was mulling over my sorry situation, I began to notice the serene looks on everyone else's faces. They were apparently used to purposelessness. I was not.

Dr. Peterson then instructed us to go off individually to contemplate. If we chose, we could do some reading and writing, but we were cautioned to avoid any form of busyness. So much for my laptop! This was a time to listen, reflect and get in touch with our inner selves. Then, Dr. Peterson explained, we would periodically come back together as a group and, under his leadership, be given further instructions and share our discoveries.

I was encouraged that at least we had a game plan. This was something I might be able to get my teeth into. We had structure. I trudged back to my room, purposefully determined to be purposeless. Okay, so old habits die hard.

I sat on the floor with no phone and no television to distract me and decided to make the best of it. Forsaking the temptation to turn on my computer, I sat in a corner, opened my Bible on my lap and silently waited with my eyes first closed, then opened and then closed. I stared alternatively at the aged patina of the beige walls and the dark insides of my eyelids. Nothing happened! After a while, I strolled through the gardens and sat cross-legged in the shade of a great tree while the birds sang to each other overhead. Their carefree twittering seemed to taunt me. I felt like a lonely discordant note within the symphony of God's creation. It took the better part of a day to slow down my mental metabolism.

I'm not sure how it started, but after an indeterminate amount of time, I began to feel like I was in a huge spiritual decompression chamber. The pace and press of the life that I had lived on a daily basis had seemed normal up to that point. After all, I'd told myself, "I am a responsible adult, and I have lots of important responsibilities." Suddenly my world began to look entirely different from the way I had understood it. I could see that my priorities had been upside down. So much of everything I did was about my need for a sense of importance. I had allowed myself to be driven by it. I felt exposed and overly consumed with self. This was deeply disconcerting.

I sat broken and ashamed amid birdsong. I reflected and repented over the manner in which I had conducted my life. After a while, I began to experience a growing awareness of God's compassion and love. Exuberance and freedom emerged from the ashes of my painful self-revelation. Shame turned to joy. I began to worship in perfect harmony with the twittering birds around me.

I had thought that the passage, "Be still, and know that I am God" (Psalm 46:10 KJV), was a command that meant, "Shut up long enough so I can talk." Consequently, I had spent years praying long fervent prayers interspersed with a few moments of silence during which I hoped God would hurry up and say something. My "active listening" skills had remained severely underdeveloped. That day in the garden I discovered that *still* means far more than closing one's mouth. It takes significant time and purposelessness to nurture a quieted soul. Stillness, I realized, is a condition that is utterly foreign to most of modern humanity.

The rest of the weekend drifted by at a wonderfully slow, purposeless pace. As we gathered and shared our reflections under Dr. Peterson's direction, I discovered a growing bond with my silent retreat partners. For a brief moment in time, we were blessed as our journeys enriched one another. The power of community blossomed.

At our closing session, I said some warm goodbyes to newfound friends and headed down the long abbey drive with an entirely different feeling about the place. A perceptive smile filled my face as I pulled onto the highway. I was amused by my former misgivings, as I mulled over my revelations from the silent retreat. I determined, for no particular purpose, to detour down a less-traveled country road on the way home. I drove slowly through the beautiful countryside as I headed back toward what I hoped would be a simpler life.

CEASE STRIVING

I knew that my gains during my silent retreat weekend would quickly fade into a pleasant memory without a change of habits. I would have to be very intentional to build upon the lessons I had learned. Responsibility is a tough taskmaster that has zero tolerance for purposelessness. Mr. Responsibility and I would have to come to terms about my future. I would have to renounce my former pattern of *idolatry.*

Idol worship is putting anything, including my real-world responsibilities, ahead of the pursuit of God. That day I began the process of tearing down the walls of my egocentric nature. These walls, unlike the stone walls of Jericho, do not crumble in a happy blast of trumpets. I knew it would be a life-long demolition project. This is the path less traveled, but it is the way that leads to an increased sensitivity to the Spirit.

This is a good time to return to the verse "Be still, and know that I am God" (Psalm 46:10 KJV). The New American Standard Version better translates "Be still" as "cease striving." There is a profound message here. Striving, which seems such a necessary part of modern living, needs to be dealt with. Striving creates stress, which hinders the inner life.

How can I cease striving and still meet all my obligations and responsibilities? It seems impossible, because modern society has placed such preeminent value on productivity and personal performance. Yet, God *commands* us to cease striving. Here is a modern conundrum: on the one hand is the glorified work ethic of today's world; on the other is the essential need to set aside adequate time for the life of the spirit.

Amazingly, this seemingly unsolvable dilemma takes care of itself when the soul is sufficiently quieted. In God's presence, we somehow know what to do and when. I firmly believe that we can be far more effective in our jobs and responsibilities when we are centered in our spirits. Spiritual clarity illumines our paths. Balance offers us the highest possible outcomes in every area of our lives.

LET THE GAMES BEGIN

In 1 Corinthians 9:25-27, Paul paints a graphic picture of his motivational exercise program: "Everyone who competes in the games exercises self-control in all things. They then do it to receive a perishable wreath, but we an imperishable. Therefore I run in such a way, as not without aim; I box in such a way, as not beating the air; but I discipline my body and make it my slave, so that, after I have preached to others, I myself will not be disqualified."

It is obvious from Paul's austere language that this is a very serious part of his daily life. Running, boxing, discipline and slavery sound like an intense regimen suitable for a triathlon! If I were trying to increase gym membership enrollments in character development, I would try to make it sound a bit more inviting. Paul is just not the kind of guy to sugarcoat anything.

Before you flee in terror from a life of unending suffering, let's dig a bit deeper. Paul uses an important phrase *twice* in his description of spiritual exercise. The words he repeats are, *in such a way*. What particular "way" is he talking about? Paul explains that he does not waste energy running in every direction and indiscriminately hitting things. His energies are expended in a far more intelligent fashion. He has a plan. He is focused. He practices a version of working smarter and not just harder.

When you enter the arena of self-improvement, it is possible, even likely, to discover that the harder you run, the further behind you get. I have this mental image of sitting in the stands of the Character Olympics and watching people running very slowly, backwards! No one ever gets to the finish line. It takes wisdom to win this race. This chapter is about directing our efforts "in such a way" that we can make meaningful progress and enjoy life at the same time.

The previous chapter exposed how the diminishment and hype of Faith, Hope and Love distort our relationship with God. They represent a major train wreck in the quest to make spiritual progress. Balanced Faith, Hope and Love are the Motivational Virtues that God uses to shape our character. They are the only means to becoming a front-runner in the Character Olympics.

The previous chapter also introduced the thought that the Spirit of God is the person who is at work to increase our Faith, Hope and Love. Let's revisit the Scriptures that support this truth and expand the life-changing concepts behind them.

> Faith: "We *through the Spirit*, by faith, are waiting" (Galatians 5:5). The Spirit is the *means* to have Faith in a confusing world.

> Hope: "That you will abound in hope *by the power of the Holy Spirit*" (Romans 15:13). The Spirit is the *multiplier* of Hope in a depressing world.

> Love: "The love of God has been poured out within our hearts *through the Holy Spirit*" (Romans 5:5). The Spirit is the *reservoir* that keeps Love flowing in an unloving world.

The Spirit is the means, the multiplier and the reservoir for Faith, Hope and Love. When I think about these statements, I realize that it would be foolish to take on the challenge of personal ch   'vel-opment by myself. I need to seriously hook up with the S source of the positive motivational power that I despere to fend off the deceptions of diminished or hyped Fait'

Let's go back to Paul's strategic words, *in such a way*. Paul also wrote the three verses above about the motivational power of the Spirit. No doubt his relationship with the Spirit was central to the "way" he ran and fought. Every other way lacks the power to succeed.

We now must face the most important question that we can ask regarding our personal development: *How can I increase my sensitivity and sense of connectedness to God's Spirit?* Fortunately, there are many successful role models to whom we can look. Many beyond Paul have successfully run the race over the last two thousand years.

For example, Dallas Willard, a leading writer in spirituality, has researched and written about historically proven "spiritual disciplines" that have helped multitudes of spiritual travelers to increase their connection with the Spirit.[1] We'll explore this idea of spiritual disciplines for the remainder of the chapter.

SPIRITUAL DISCIPLINES

We have established that the Spirit is the power source for the motivational forces of Faith, Hope and Love. Personal growth happens best when we connect and cooperate with the activity of the Holy Spirit. He has an agenda, and we are on it! He keeps us in the power zone.

Spiritual exercises or practices, on their own, have no inherent significance. Richard Foster puts their value into perspective when he calls them "our little practices," which must be enveloped by God.[2] We can't make God do anything. The rigorous exercises of prayer, study, meditation and fasting do nothing to impress God. Why? He is already deeply in love with you. He is your biggest fan. There is not one thing you can do to improve that reality. God loves you like you are, and he is wholly committed to your personal development.

We are sentient and spiritual creatures. This is what makes humankind unique from the animal kingdom. These are the two things hat make us human. There are few things sadder than seeing ⁻ne lose their sentient powers. My wife is a marketing director for an Alzheimer's and dementia care community. It is tragic to see formerly accomplished people lose all cognitive awareness.

But there is a far worse human condition than the loss of sentience. It is the loss of spirituality. The most horrific reality is to see mentally alert people who, at the end of life, are devoid of spirit.

Modern society worships sentience and largely abandons matters of the spirit. Most people live like sentient animals, out of touch with the biggest part of their humanity. Why this spirit-deadness? We possess the nature of our rebellious, ancient ancestors. Like Adam and Eve, our natural disposition is alienated from the Spirit. We relish in the flesh. The fact that we have any spiritual inclination is evidence that God is at work to awaken our humanity. We are sharp of mind and dull of spirit. This is why we need to regularly practice spiritual exercises. They serve to wake us up to our truest inner selves.

The spiritual disciplines change *us* in ways that make *us* more receptive to the Spirit. This is their value. We are the problem, not God. The regular practice of spiritual disciplines puts us in a place where we're capable of connecting with the power source, should he show up to the dance. The good news is that he loves to dance with us! James Houston reminds us, "The Holy Spirit is the person who makes the presence of God a living experience."[3] There must be a Spirit encounter if we are to live in the power zone.

Spiritual disciplines have proven to be helpful in the development of a person's character in many ways. Willard notes, "A major service of the spiritual disciplines is to cause the duplicity and malice that are buried in our will and character to surface and be dealt with."[4] This is a keen insight. We are not naturally prepared for God time. We need to get in shape for it. Let's face it: we are messed-up, self-centered, deceptive creatures who perpetually spin things to our advantage.

The Bible exposes us: "The heart is more deceitful than all else and is desperately sick; Who can understand it?" (Jeremiah 17:9). This is why we need prep time to face a holy God. Spiritual exercise can put our hearts into a condition where they are capable of engaging the Spirit.[5]

CATEGORIZING THE SPIRITUAL DISCIPLINES

The study of spiritual disciplines has been around for a very long time. Some of the spiritual disciplines listed below are commonly practiced today. Others may appear to be strange—right out of the Dark Ages. They represent concepts that are less obvious but are worthy of exploration. You do not need to be a cloistered monk to participate in these exercises of the soul. They work equally well for a gardener, priest, busy parent or CEO.

Many of the disciplines that have proven to be helpful in the past have been categorized in different and interesting ways. Richard Foster organizes the common ones into the categories of Inward, Outward and Corporate.[6] Dallas Willard breaks them into the categories of Disciplines of Abstinence and Disciplines of Engagement. He calls them "the outbreathing and inbreathing of our spiritual lives."[7] Willard's list of fifteen disciplines is outlined in figure 5.1.[8]

COMMON SPIRITUAL DISCIPLINES	
DISCIPLINES OF ABSTINENCE	DISCIPLINES OF ENGAGEMENT
Solitude	Study
Silence	Worship
Fasting	Celebration
Frugality	Service
Chastity	Prayer
Secrecy	Fellowship
Sacrifice	Confession
	Submission

Figure 5.1

Each of these items represents a different character-building exercise. A strong word of caution is in order here. It would be foolhardy for anyone to attempt an exercise regimen that includes all of the fifteen spiritual disciplines just listed. Imagine visiting a gym and doing several rounds on every exercise machine the first day. You would probably be unable to walk the following day.

Spiritual disciplines apply to different people, with different needs, in different circumstances, at different times. John Ortberg shares the story of how he attempted an overly aggressive approach to spiritual exercise and gave up in total discouragement.[9] Foster warns, "It is a common mistake to assume that if we will only do enough spiritual practice, our efforts will result in a satisfying spiritual life."[10] We must carefully evaluate which spiritual discipline, or mix of disciplines, is appropriate for our personal development at any given time.

SPIRITUAL PRACTICES AND THE MOTIVATIONAL VIRTUES

The Motivational Virtues present a very different way to categorize the list of Willard's fifteen spiritual disciplines. I see God's character-building gym with three main workout areas. Some exercises do more to strengthen the area of our Faith, others do more to build our Hope, and still others increase our Love.

Next to each spiritual practice in the list below is an abbreviated description of how that particular exercise can impact the development of one of the Motivational Virtues. In the next chapter these descriptions are significantly expanded and applied to the process of making spiritual progress. We do well to keep in mind that nothing in the way of spiritual transformation can happen without the activity of the Spirit.

Faith

Solitude: Trusting God's sufficiency

Silence: Trusting God's voice

Study: Apprehending truth in Scripture

Prayer: Apprehending God in life

Submission: Trusting God in relationships

Hope

Fasting: Delayed gratification of the body

Frugality: Delayed gratification of the soul

Secrecy: Anticipation of ultimate disclosure

Sacrifice: Delayed gratification of desire

Service: Anticipation of reward

Love

Chastity: Intimacy with man

Worship: Intimacy with God

Celebration: Intimacy with God and man

Fellowship: Intimate friendship with God and man

Confession: Intimate humility with God and man

COMMON MISCONCEPTIONS ABOUT
THE SPIRITUAL DISCIPLINES

We need to fully understand our part in the pursuit of good character. This is a good time to clarify some common misconceptions that people have about the spiritual disciplines. This is important because spiritual exercises, done incorrectly, provide no benefits to the practitioner.

God on a hook. Exercising spiritual disciplines does not obligate God nor does it *earn* special consideration from God. We have no hook with which to manipulate him. Our relationship with him is totally on the basis of grace—undeserved favor. We can do nothing to earn more of his favor. The purpose of all spiritual disciplines is to simply put oneself in the position to hear what God is saying. He decides when and if he wants to speak.

Lucky encounters. Spiritual disciplines remind me of Samuel Goldwyn's classic adage, "The harder I work the luckier I get." Benjamin Franklin put it this way: "Diligence is the mother of good luck." Discipline, spiritual or otherwise, has nothing to do with luck but has everything to do with putting ourselves in a position for good things to happen. Stated another way, spiritual disciplines increase the likelihood (not to be confused with luck) of experiencing transforming face times with God.

Watch me. There are few things more insufferable than talking to people who are proud of a spiritual discipline they have mastered. There is no room for pride here. It is no spiritual accomplishment to establish a routine of getting up at five o'clock every morning to read the Word and pray. Other people get up earlier every day to take care of the baby, get the kids' lunches ready for school or go to work. Routines are meaningless in and of themselves. Spiritual disciplines are not an end in and of themselves. They keep us ever humble as we daily demonstrate an utter dependency on Christ and the power of his presence. We do well to recall that the agenda of the Spirit through the practice of all our spiritual exercises is to build our character by causing us to increase in Faith, Hope and Love. We miss the mark and suffer a disconnect with God when we try to advance our own agenda.

One size fits all. When we are feeling good about ourselves, we have an aggravating tendency to tell other people that they need to do what we are doing. John Ortberg writes, "We need the freedom to discover how God wants us to grow, for His design will not look quite the same for everyone."[11] This is true because not all people have the same character issues. Cooperating with the Holy Spirit will require different spiritual disciplines for different people at different times. For one person, it may mean learning to stop and listen through the regular practices of solitude, meditation and reflection. For another, it may mean establishing a regimen of prayer or fasting or devotional readings in the Scriptures. The Spirit may convict an individual of a specific need to engage in the less-practiced disciplines of sacrificial serving or of connecting with others more fully in community.

MOTIVATIONS

It is necessary to discuss the matter of motivations when talking about spiritual exercise. The wrong motive can derail your efforts before you start. People can spend years dutifully following a spiritual exercise regimen to no avail. I list some of the more common misdirected motives below.

Personal advancement. At first glance this seems like a great motive. What is wrong with wanting to achieve your greatest potential? It is possible that this could be the end result of faithful exercise, but it is the wrong starting point. We must approach God selflessly. He is worthy of serving even if we never receive any benefits from it. True worship is always about giving and not getting. When seeking God, we must leave the ultimate results to him.

Personal debasement. Depending on your perspective, this might look like a lofty, selfless goal, but there's one problem. God wants to move us beyond repentance. He created us for friendship. His objective is to build us up and not to tear us down. He wants to put confidence in our step and a smile on our face. We are sons and daughters of the King, who are destined to rule and reign with him. God is building disciples who can showcase powerful, restored humanity, not broken, pathetic souls who continually feel unworthy of God's forgiveness and restoration.

Mystical experiences. People want to feel special and unique. Nothing could feel more exclusive than having a personal visitation from God that you could brag about to your friends. "God told me!" is the coinage of this realm. The driving motivation originates from a lack of personal significance. God is not in the habit of inflating our pride. He does not want to be a stuffed trophy on our wall. He does want to heal our sense of insignificance and make us whole and secure with his unconditional love.

Spiritual highs. Spirituality, in some circles, is defined in emotional terms. This can lead people to "feel" close to God one moment and very far away the next. Like an addict, they're always looking for the next high. Encounters with the Spirit are not about getting an emotional fix. The net effect of an encounter with the Spirit may actually be an "emotional" downer. God may expose our inner condition to the point that we fall on our faces and wail in remorse. Brokenness later bears the fruit of purified character. God is not interested in fixing our fickle feelings but in fixing our everlasting soul.

Special power. There are people who are inappropriately enamored with miracles and the supernatural. You might call them miracle groupies. The Bible records the story of a man named Simon who was captivated by the miracles that he observed in the lives of the apostles. He offered them money to have that same power. They reproved him for his impure motives: "Your heart is not right before God. . . . You are in the . . . bondage of iniquity" (Acts 8:21-23).

So what is the right motive behind the practice of the spiritual disciplines? It is simple. The right motive is a sincere love for Christ with a desire to be close to him and to please him with the anticipation of nothing in return. He is worthy.

FINAL THOUGHTS

We need to establish spiritual disciplines and order our lives in a way that will increase the likelihood of experiencing face times with God. We must do so with adequate humility and patience without expectations. We are only responsible for our part. God is always faithful, in his time, to come through on his part. Tozer reminds us of God's perpetual inclination: "Our pursuit of God is successful just because He is forever seeking to manifest Himself to us."[12]

God is not obligated to respond to incantations, formulas like "in the name of Jesus," sacrifices, outbursts of frustration, orders, presumptions or any other forms of manipulation. He never owes us an appearance. God always appears according to *his* schedule. He is never late but always arrives precisely when he intends to. Speaking about the Spirit, John declared, "The wind blows where it wishes" (John 3:8). God cannot be tamed. We need to be.

God avoids habitual codependencies, like taking our responsibilities into his own hands. He works on our hearts and minds but leaves the ultimate decisions to us. We have to make the choice to become spiritually active. God knows that the exercise of our free will is integral to the development of our character.

The world has seen enough spiritually flabby, out-of-condition Christians who do not give a good showing of the transformational power of Christ. The "light of the world," of which Jesus spoke in Matthew 5:14, is the intense brilliance of transformed character. It supersedes anything that can be said to advance the cause of Christ. The world needs to see power from the power zone. Nothing compares to the shine of Faith-filled, Hope-filled and Love-filled people in the midst of darkness. It is time to pursue a spiritual exercise regimen in earnest.

6

CHANGING YOUR TREE
How God Grows People

> To conquer oneself is the best and noblest victory;
> to be vanquished by one's own nature is
> the worst and most ignoble defeat.
>
> Plato

> Then the Spirit of the LORD will come
> upon you mightily, and you shall . . .
> be changed into another man.
>
> 1 Samuel 10:6

The first rule of personal motivation, at the beginning of chapter one, introduced the principle of cause and effect. This principle can be observed as a proven reality throughout nature: bad tree—bad fruit; good tree—good fruit. How can a bad tree produce good fruit? Jesus offered one potential possibility in the verses below. The solution goes to the very core of our being. We need to acquire a new tree. We need a new nature.

The principle of cause and effect: "So every good tree bears

e bad tree bears bad fruit. A good tree cannot

it, nor can a bad tree produce good fruit"

.

...iraculous possibility: "Either make the tree good and its fruit good, or make the tree bad and its fruit bad; for the tree is known by its fruit" (Matthew 12:33).

These verses represent two profound truths that are foundational to making spiritual progress: (1) We cannot change our fruit; but (2) We *can* change our tree. This chapter is about tree changing.

Long ago God confronted bad character with sobering words that illustrate the principle of cause and effect. "Can the Ethiopian change his skin or the leopard his spots? Then you also can do good who are accustomed to doing evil" (Jeremiah 13:23). This is a rhetorical question. The answer is *no*, of course! We can't change our spots. We are what we are.

Jesus, as we have seen, taught another path. We can change our "tree." It is not quick and easy. Spiritual growth is no trivial matter. It requires nothing less than a recoding of our spiritual DNA. A leopard can become as white as snow. A thorn bush can be miraculously transformed into an apple tree. How is this accomplished?

For starters, you have no shortage of options when it comes to personal growth choices. A Google search for "self-improvement" returns over 86 million hits. It's no surprise that people wonder where to start. It seems that there is a motivational/character fitness expert on every corner.

As we have seen throughout the book, God is committed to our personal growth. It makes sense that God, our Creator, would be the unequalled expert on personal growth. That's why it is wise to begin our quest by asking, "How does God grow people?"

Is God's approach really that different from every other approach? If so, how? Let's begin our journey in that direction.

THE ACTIVITY OF GOD

Believe it or not, God is not primarily focused on changing our haviors. He is not a serial behavior changer. This is one of the uniqu things about the way God grows people. Behaviors are merely *symptoms* of an inner motivational condition of the heart. God knows that when our motivations change, our behaviors automatically change. The Spirit is actively at work to change our motivations. This is ground zero for the activity of God.

"Changing our tree" is all about changing our motivational core. It means that we must cultivate and grow in Faith, Hope and Love. This is not an effortless process because, as we have seen, there is some stiff competition for our motivations. The lust of the flesh, lust of the eyes and the pride of life vie for our attention and threaten to pull us out of the balance of the power zone, the region where the DNA of our character becomes recoded through the miraculous workings of God's Spirit. How can we keep growing and prevail over the forces that threaten to make us imbalanced, dysfunctional people? We must avail ourselves of all of God's provisions if we are to make optimal spiritual progress in Faith, Hope or Love.

PREPARING THE SOIL FOR CHANGING YOUR TREE

Socrates is widely regarded as one of the great thinkers in world history. He made a provocative statement over 2,400 years ago that is still relevant today: "The unexamined life is not worth living." The urgency of these ancient words resonates with the modern investigative mind. Self-discovery, for many, is truly the last undiscovered frontier.

Modern technological marvels have taught us a vast amount about our physical universe. The Hubble Space Telescope has given us unimagined glimpses of far-flung galaxies and striking images of colorful nebulae. The Kepler space observatory has revealed the existence of many planets surrounding faraway suns. A recent headline reported, "World's Largest Atom Smasher May Have Detected 'God

s quest for discovery reaches across the span
nd down to the level of subatomic particles.
of the physical universe, the human race
...are of spiritual realities.

...om ultimately comes from an all-knowing God. Humankind's great discoveries are simply the uncovering of things that the
Creator has embedded within the workings of his universe. The
passion to learn and grow is something that God has placed within
us. The Bible confirms the urgency of Socrates's inner exploratory
wisdom: "But a man must examine himself. . . . But if we judged
ourselves rightly, we would not be judged" (1 Corinthians 11:28, 31).
Self-examination is *not* optional for a conscientious soul.

Why is it so important to examine ourselves? The true state of our
inner being is not intuitive to us. It is a land of discovery. We will need
help if we are to plumb the depths of our hearts. God knows that we
are tricky beings. Just under the surface we discover false self-messages,
layers of duplicity, self-justifying defense systems, unresolved pain,
neediness and denial, to name a few of humanity's foibles.

With hearts like this, why do we neglect to examine ourselves?
Inertia is understandable. It is easier to be who we are than who we
can become. It is more comfortable to practice avoidance than to
work through what feels like difficult internal issues. A lot of the time
we are just too busy living life to own a well-lived life. Busyness often
comes at the severe expense of personal blindness and perpetuated
dysfunction. If we are going to be successful in changing our tree, we
are going to have to dig deep and stir up the hardened soil that comes
from an unexamined life.

TWO PREEMINENT RESOURCES FOR CHANGING YOUR TREE

Contrary to every other approach, God's method for growing people
involves his direct activity in our lives. Unfortunately, we are not

always listening or receptive to his faithful interventions. There a₁
two primary means that God uses to change our tree: the Word and
the Spirit of God. J. I. Packer calls them "parallel figures. God's Word
is His almighty speech; God's Spirit is His almighty breath."²

Both the Word of God and the Spirit of God represent an incalculable investment by God toward humanity. His Word is the investment of thousands of years of engaging and speaking to people
who were often resistant to his voice and purposes. His Spirit is the
culmination of Christ's costly, sacrificial death on the cross. He paid
the price for *our* sins. The righteousness of Christ, accessible through
Faith, bridged the chasm between a holy God and sinful people.
God's holiness was extended to us by Faith. This set the stage for God
to make a huge down payment on our behalf.

What down payment? The Spirit! Paul tells the exciting tale:
"Having also believed, you were sealed in Him with the Holy Spirit of
promise, who is given as a pledge of our inheritance" (Ephesians 1:13-
14). The Spirit is given as a *pledge*, literally a down payment, that God
will fulfill all the rest of his future promises. It is impossible to imagine
a bigger pledge or down payment by God toward our spiritual progress.

THREE PRINCIPLES FOR SPIRITUAL GROWTH

We have seen that changing our tree requires the work of the Word
and the Spirit. Now we'll examine three essential contexts that fa-
cilitate this growth.

*Tree-changing principle number one: Growing in the context of
God's Spirit.* We need to engage the Spirit because the Spirit is en-
gaging us. John writes of the ministry of God's Spirit in the life of the
Christian: "I will ask the Father, and He will give you another Helper,
that He may be with you forever" (John 14:16). Note the word *another*.
Packer observes that this is "because Jesus was the original Comforter,
and the newcomer's task was to continue this side of His ministry."³
The Greek word for "Helper" literally means "advocate" or "sup-

·it becomes our lifelong constant companion in
\al growth. This is a far deeper relationship than
..̇ket sitting on our shoulder. We are not just convicted of
sin; but he is our intimate guide, like Jesus was with his earthly disciples.[5] This is why Dallas Willard calls spiritual formation a "Spirit-driven process."[6] How can I *grow* in Faith, Hope and Love? Let's look at the second context for making spiritual progress.

Tree-changing principle number two: Growing in the context of God's speech. Rick Warren reminds us of the powerful ministry of the Word: "The Bible is far more than a doctrinal guidebook."[7] It has the power to expose the motives of our hearts and simultaneously change them. Of course, this will not do much good if we are not regularly engaged with the Word as an integral part of our devotional life.[8]

When you regularly engage the Bible, it's like watching your portrait emerge on a canvas. You are exposed by the revealing strokes of a master Artist. A mosaic of truth emerges. "Line on line, a little here, a little there. Indeed, He will speak to this people" (Isaiah 28:10-11). You can't absorb it all at once. Nor are you intended to. It's too powerful. You need small digestible portions. Frequency matters. Continual exposure sharpens our inner sensitivities. It is a honing process like slowly drawing a blade against a whetting stone.

God's Word is like the manna that sustained ancient Israel during their forty-year sojourn in the desert. They had to consume it daily. Stale bread does not nourish a soul.

The Bible is the only source of spiritual truth that is 100 percent accurate. Long ago, King David gave us what could be called the absolute equation: "The sum of Your word is truth" (Psalm 119:160). It is *absolute* truth. The Bible's cumulative effect eradicates false thinking and self-deception.

The Bible records an ancient tradition when spiritual leaders brought clarity to God's Word. The Levites of ancient Israel did so almost 2,500 years ago. "They read from the Book of the Law of God, making it clear and giving the meaning so that the people understood what was being read" (Nehemiah 8:8 NIV). This is the impact of a well-presented modern sermon.

There is also a lot to be said for the benefits of daily devotionals that apply God's Word to our lives. This is particularly true if the devotionals target our specific growth areas, like the ones at Spiritual Progress.com. The busyness of life makes it often helpful to have the wonders of God's Word unpacked for us. "The unfolding of Your words gives light; It gives understanding to the simple" (Psalm 119:130). God's Word penetrates. It's like an ultrasound for the soul.

We are assaulted on a daily basis with multitudes of false messages that urge us to spend our money and make choices that are not in our best interests. We need regular doses of truth to counter them. We need more than just right thinking; we need right motivations. This is not always readily apparent to us. "All the ways of a man are clean in his own sight, But the LORD weighs the motives" (Proverbs 16:2).

The Bible is not just a book of moral ideals. Rather, it surgically exposes our underlying motivations. "For the word of God is living and active and sharper than any two-edged sword, and piercing as far as the division of soul and spirit, of both joints and marrow, and able to judge the thoughts and intentions of the heart" (Hebrews 4:12). The Bible is a book that exposes false motivations and generates positive ones. It disassembles falsehood and compels us to grow to our greatest potential. The Bible is a spiritual mirror. "For if anyone is a hearer of the word . . . he is like a man who looks at his natural face in a mirror" (James 1:23). When we peer into its perfection we see ourselves as we truly are. The mirror of the Scriptures, like all mirrors, serves to expose the naked truth. It shows us a measure of ourselves that is impossible to grasp in any other way.

Actors use mirrors to see imperfections as they practice the performance of their character. My teenaged daughters quickly became intimately acquainted with mirrors. Mirrors provide immediate feedback. The effects of each minor adjustment can be instantly measured. Few women would imagine putting on much makeup without the reliable feedback of a mirror.

Why do we think spiritual improvement is any different? In the absence of a mirror, a makeover becomes a mess. James used the analogy of a mirror because it describes the Bible's critical role in our personal development. The makeup of our character becomes unknowingly smeared when we neglect to peer into the Bible's flawless reflection. Often, everyone can see the smudge but us. Our inattention puts a burden on friends to point out our character issues. Many are not up to the task. Our growth languishes. Continued character issues never get addressed and often become more pronounced. This is an unintended consequence of the unexamined life.

Mirrors have one severe limitation. Not long after we walk away, it becomes increasingly difficult to remember the image we beheld. A mirror's insight is temporary. James put it this way: "For once he has looked at himself and gone away, he has immediately forgotten what kind of person he was" (James 1:24). This truth makes us mirror-dependent. No one can make spiritual progress when navigating blindly. We are Word-dependent.

The power of the Scriptures and the Spirit that illumines them are at the heart of how God grows people. In previous chapters, we have examined ourselves in the light of the motivational forces of Faith, Hope and Love. We have also peered into the dark stagnant bogs of the lust of the flesh, the lust of the eyes and the pride of life and seen a measure of ourselves there. These reflecting pools of the Scriptures, both good and evil, offer insights that are foundational to our spiritual growth. They provide a framework for understanding our character and the motivations that drive us. This enables us to make spiritual progress in an enlightened and informed way.

Tree-changing principle number three: Growing in the context of community. The journey to making spiritual progress is both a lonely, quiet path and a bustling, noisy highway. Self-examination involves highly personal times of deep reflection and painfully loud criticisms of others. God uses both. Life in the Spirit involves stillness in isolated green pastures and disturbing intrusions from a clamoring world. Engaging the Word involves silent insights of surgical precision and visual actions of obedience in our relationships. Try as we might, the spiritual life is not a solo journey. Spiritual progress demands that we involve others on our journey. We must learn to be transparent with God and our fellow human companions.

There are few things more helpful to our spiritual progress than the presence of close friends who will tell us the straight truth about ourselves. They are a cherished blessing from God. People see things in our lives that are almost impossible for us to see on our own.

The Spirit may have been trying to open our eyes to our problem. The Word may have been speaking to our issue. The black inked words we needed have been right in front of us. But sometimes we are too spiritually dull to see and hear what God is saying. That's where people with flesh and blood come in. They are harder to ignore. We do well to listen. Friend or foe, they are emissaries of God.

We need dependable friends who care about us enough to confront our shortcomings. The last thing we need is to be surrounded by disingenuous people who always tell us what we want to hear. The ancient wisdom of Proverbs speaks to this exact situation: "Faithful are the wounds of a friend, but deceitful are the kisses of an enemy" (Proverbs 27:6). This ancient verse is reminiscent of a colloquial phrase used to describe insincere, flattering friends today. They are aptly called "kiss ups." Who needs friends like this? They are enemies of the welfare of our souls. I would much rather be insulted by someone who cares about me than complimented by someone with questionable motives.

The Bible makes it a real priority to have others involved in the development of our character. Paul's language in Ephesians 4:15 instructs us on how to engage others in our spiritual progress and gives us the two critical ingredients for growth: "But speaking the truth in love, we are to grow up in all aspects into Him who is the head, even Christ" (Ephesians 4:15).

Speaking the truth without Love is self-absorption. Love without truth is deception. True friends bring the twin bright lights of truth and love into our lives. They help us to remain in the power zone of Faith, Hope and Love.

SPIRITUAL EXERCISES FOR SPIRITUAL GROWTH

Up to this point we have looked at the *contexts* for making spiritual progress—that is, *in* the Spirit, *in* the Word and *in* community. Now we must explore the *practices* for making spiritual progress. In the previous chapter we briefly examined several of the traditional spiritual disciplines and their ability to cause growth in the areas of Faith, Hope and Love. You could say that they represent God's character-building gym.

Everyone can participate in the following exercise regimen. Even a busy mom, dad, young adult or student can learn to create short intervals of devotion that have life-changing impacts. Just be careful to not overdo it. When it comes to spiritual exercise, more is not always better. The Spirit will lead you as you develop the unique workout regimen that is right for you. Let's dig deeper to better understand how these exercises can help us to make spiritual progress.

FIVE SPIRITUAL PRACTICES TO GROW IN FAITH

Solitude: Trusting God's sufficiency. Solitude is the practice of getting alone and away from all potential interruptions for the specific purpose of quieting our souls. It can be a very scary place. We are likely to meet God and certain to meet ourselves. It frees us from the hectic pace of modern living. Jesus practiced it regularly: "After He had sent the crowds away, He went up on the mountain by Himself to pray; and when it was evening, He was there alone" (Matthew 14:23). Aloneness removes the distractions and interactions that can mask our inner fears. Solitude brings us face-to-face with our insecurities. We cry out to God. Stripped of false dependencies, Faith blossoms.

Silence: *Trusting God's voice.* Silence is often combined with the practice of solitude. Silence is different in that it changes us from noisemakers to listeners. "Be still, and know that I am God" (Psalm 46:10 KJV). Often the shortest path to stillness is to simply shut our mouths. Talking is a form of busyness that masks many inner issues. Silence, as a spiritual practice, puts us in an abject state of dependency. We are incapable of pleading our side of things. We can say nothing to change our circumstances. As we silently listen, Faith blossoms.

Study: *Apprehending truth in Scripture.* The regular practice of exploring God's Word opens us up to God's active voice. It counters the many false messages that surround us with spiritual truth. Truth is liberating. Paul knew the power of it: "So faith comes from hearing, and hearing by the word of Christ" (Romans 10:17). When we receive regular doses of truth, all of life begins to make sense to us. Hearing God's voice causes us to know him. Knowing God causes us to trust him. When we trust him, Faith blossoms!

Prayer: *Apprehending God in life.* Prayer, as a spiritual practice, is worship and trust in God. It is not talking to God as an outsider. "But you, beloved, building yourselves up on your most holy faith, praying in the Holy Spirit" (Jude 1:20). Prayer is fellowship with the Spirit. Jesus taught us how to pray. Before we get to the asking part, Jesus showed us the portals of surrender that all must go through. "Pray, then, in this way: Our Father who is in heaven. . . . Your kingdom come. Your will be done, On earth as it is in heaven" (Matthew 6:9-10). The prayer of Faith trusts and surrenders to the goodness of an all-wise God. When we pray rightly, Faith blossoms.

Submission: Trusting God in relationships. Submission is a spiritual exercise that takes an advanced level of trust. It can be manifested through many forms of self-denial. In extreme cases it refuses to take up a sword and declares, "I put my trust in God." The ancient truth spoken to Jehoshaphat still holds true: "The battle is not yours but God's" (2 Chronicles 20:15). Submission is a discipline of spirit that holds strong when the flesh screams for justice or retaliation. Jesus taught, "Whoever forces you to go one mile, go with him two" (Matthew 5:41). Why? Every step of the second mile is a smiling expression of your free will. When you submit to an unruly boss, it is not your boss winning. It is Faith winning in you.

FIVE SPIRITUAL PRACTICES TO GROW IN HOPE

Fasting: Delayed gratification of the body. The spiritual practice of fasting is an exercise of self-denial from all sorts of earthly desires. It is typically linked to food but may include seasons of abstinence from entertainments or even relationships. Fasting is a form of self-denial that says a direct "no!" to the Flesh and "yes!" to the Spirit. It chokes off false fleshly hopes very close to the ground. It is not some extreme thing done to impress God, but a humbling of the flesh. Fasting is exclusively for the sake of improving one's spiritual focus or vision. Quieted flesh means increased spiritual sensitivity. Hope increases when we say no to basic desires and yes to God.

Frugality: Delayed gratification of the soul. The spiritual practice of frugality intentionally rejects all forms of material excess. The rich and poor can equally practice it. It takes a minimalist approach toward life. This is not because material things are necessarily evil, but because "things" can be a huge distraction from right priorities. The Bible exhorts, "Make sure that your character is free from the love of money, being content with what you have" (Hebrews 13:5). Frugality trades in the possibilities of a better present for a much grander future. It stores treasures in heaven. Hope increases when we reject present gratifications in anticipation of future glory.

Secrecy: Anticipation of ultimate disclosure. The spiritual practice of secrecy strips all self-promoting motives out of our devotions to God. Pride is a deadly enemy of the Motivational Virtue of Hope. It is the trickiest of evils. Just when we begin to compliment ourselves on our spiritual advancement, we realize that pride has somehow slipped in the back door and reinserted its ugly self. Secrecy is an informed response to a warning given by Jesus: "Beware of practicing your righteousness before men to be noticed by them; otherwise you have no reward with your Father who is in heaven" (Matthew 6:1). Hope increases when we worship and serve in secret.

Sacrifice: Delayed gratification of desire. The spiritual practice of sacrifice is not focused on the sacrifice. Nor is it focused on self-achievement. Done rightly, it is a humble exercise of worship to God. It is not extreme behavior reserved only for the intensely religious. Paul advocated it as normative behavior. "Present your bodies a living and holy sacrifice, acceptable to God, which is your spiritual service of worship" (Romans 12:1). The costliest sacrifice knows it is still getting a great deal. Today's "momentary, light affliction is producing for us an eternal weight of glory far beyond all comparison" (2 Corinthians 4:17). And "if we endure, we will also reign with Him" (2 Timothy 2:12). Costly acts of personal sacrifice build our Hope.

Service: Anticipation of reward. The spiritual practice of service is a form of spiritual intelligence. Only low-Hope people are shortsighted enough to exclusively serve themselves. Jesus used an example of a most mundane, unimpressive act of service to make a poignant point. "Whoever in the name of a disciple gives to one of these little ones even a cup of cold water to drink, truly I say to you, he shall not lose his reward" (Matthew 10:42). If a simple, free act of kindness like that guarantees a reward, imagine what a life dedicated to serving others could produce! A heightened level of worshipful service builds awareness of the promises of Hope.

FIVE SPIRITUAL PRACTICES TO GROW IN LOVE

Chastity (love): Intimacy with humankind. Love is a Motivational Virtue but it is also a spiritual practice. It is something that gets better with practice. Love requires practical choices, choosing to put the interests of others ahead of its own desires. This practice is best epitomized in the choice that Christ made when he gave his life for us. "Who gave Himself for our sins so that He might rescue us from this present evil age" (Galatians 1:4). Jesus challenged us to make the same Love choice: "Greater love has no one than this, that one lay down his life for his friends" (John 15:13). Love grows when loving choices are made.

Worship: Intimacy with God. The practice of worship is central to the spiritual life. The need for this practice may appear to be self-evident, but many believers sorely neglect to exercise it. It's easy to take God's blessings and Love for granted. Reduced worship always indicates detached intimacy with God. Passionate worship is evidence of a heart that has embraced the first and greatest commandment: "You shall love the Lord your God with all your heart, and with all your soul, and with all your strength, and with all your mind" (Luke 10:27). Worship rightly aligns the heart with God. Where there is great Love, there is great worship.

Celebration: Intimacy with God and humankind. The spiritual practice of celebration is group worship. This spiritual practice is impossible to do alone. The people of God have a lot to celebrate. Celebration gatherings of the flock have been going on since antiquity. They are an integral part of being the people of God. Why do so many people of faith today neglect this vital spiritual practice? The Bible commands its observance: "Not forsaking our own assembling together, as is the habit of some, but encouraging one another" (Hebrews 10:25). The Bible describes amazing scenes of group celebrations in heaven. Are you ready for a group experience? Celebration excites the heart and reminds us that we are not alone on our journey. Celebration builds new dimensions of our Love.

Fellowship: Intimate friendship with God and humankind. The practice of fellowship is a relational commitment to God and to others. Again, this spiritual practice is impossible to do alone. The truth is that we need each other to make spiritual progress in the area of Love. It is easy to imagine you're a saint when stranded on a deserted island, but God develops our character through interactions with others. We see dimensions of our self that can be gained in no other way. This is the only path where "the love of each one of you toward one another grows ever greater" (2 Thessalonians 1:3). Solomon described this principle in action: "Iron sharpens iron, so one man sharpens another" (Proverbs 27:17). God uses the sparks that fly from human encounters to both illumine and shape our character. Where spiritual friendships flourish, Love grows.

Confession: Intimate humility with God and humankind. Confession is a spiritual practice that takes our relationships with others to an entirely new place. It involves a level of transparency and vulnerability that is foreign to this world. Confession is regarded as weakness to outsiders. In God's kingdom, the humble shall be exalted. Confession is Love on steroids. This practice belongs exclusively to people of faith. It releases the healing power of God in our hearts and in the lives of others. Find an inner circle of community in which you are comfortable practicing confession. Don't neglect this practice! "Confess your sins to one another, and pray for one another so that you may be healed" (James 5:16). Confession keeps the heart open for deeper levels of Love.

FINAL THOUGHTS

God has a plan to help you to overrule the principle of cause and effect in your life. He wants to miraculously change your tree. He has invested heavily to make it possible. He wants to fill you with Faith, Hope and Love so that your underlying motivations are transformed. He wants to give you the kind of balanced character that reflects the spiritual reality of salvation: "If anyone is in Christ, he is a new creature; the old things passed away; behold, new things have come" (2 Corinthians 5:17).

Making spiritual progress is a progressive work by a committed and faithful God. The apostle Paul was excited about the divine process: "For I am confident of this very thing, that He who began a good work in you will perfect it until the day of Christ Jesus" (Philippians 1:6). God wants to take you in and keep you in the power zone where you are under the influence of his Spirit.

All that remains is a determined commitment on your part to make spiritual progress. The objective is attainable. You will need to learn how to abide in the contexts of the Spirit, the Word and community. You will also need to find and keep adjusting the right spiritual workout practices that best meet your needs.

In addition to spiritual insight and knowledge, you will need an accurate spiritual assessment to find your starting point. Once you discover your motivational growth areas, you are able to understand yourself better and know how to most effectively make spiritual progress. This is the subject of the concluding chapter. Before then, there is much more to learn about the motivations that shape our character: Faith, Hope and Love.

FAITH

The Trusting Virtue

> *Every tomorrow has two handles.*
> *We can take hold of it with the handle*
> *of anxiety or the handle of faith.*
>
> Henry Beecher

> *Without faith it is impossible to please Him.*
>
> Hebrews 11:6

Loud cracks of rapid gunfire interrupted my evening teaching, mid-sentence. I had been speaking on the subject of prayer. We were about to move from theory to practice in a big way.

No, I had not been crazy enough to take a missions trip into a dangerous country engaged in a civil war. The enemy had brought the war to our doorstep. It was a Sunday evening at our church in prosperous Bellevue, Washington. We were a scant three miles from Microsoft's main campus, in the center of a very upscale community.

At the first sound of gunfire, a few church leaders immediately jumped to their feet and rushed out the doors to assess the situation. Some headed to check on and secure our children who were under the supervision of our children's pastor and her staff in the gymnasium on the other side of the campus. Some made 911 calls on their cell phones. A deacon positioned himself at the sanctuary doors to relay information to us inside.

As the lead pastor I stayed in the worship center and instructed the remainder of the congregation to stay with me, lest in panic someone run into harm's way. I assured everyone that the situation was being monitored and that competent friends would quickly report back and we would take appropriate action. As I spoke, we could hear bullets hitting the side of the worship center wall. I asked the congregation to lie down to reduce our profile and to pray for God's hand of protection.

What happened next is difficult to explain. A sense of God's presence filled the room. Faith blossomed. The peace of God settled over our hearts in an inexplicable way. No one panicked. We lay on the floor and prayed. The tape from that night records the sound of gunfire in the background as I led a calm congregation in prayer over the microphone.

Our minds were foremost on the welfare of our kids. I knew there were other parents, like me, who had to resist the temptation to give in to fear. This was one of those moments when circumstances were beyond our control and we had to trust God completely. Amazingly, trust became effortless. Peace ruled over the terror of evil.

The report soon came back from one of our deacons that the children were all unharmed. "Everyone is fine," he said with a sigh of relief. "They have been moved to a safe area, the lights have been turned off, and they are lying on the floor."

I led a prayer that God by his Spirit would pacify the shooter. This was a church meeting where I knew everyone was praying. We interceded for the gunman. We prayed that the demonic force that held him under its influence would be bound by God's Spirit. We continued to pray in earnest knowing the situation could take a very dangerous or fatal turn at any moment. The shooter was obviously deranged. The sharp reports of gunfire started up again.

The welcome sound of sirens wailed in the distance as police units were racing to our location from every quadrant of the city. We all knew that a person would soon be shot, as the police were getting closer. Someone was going to die on our church campus unless God intervened. I felt directed to pray that the gunman would cease shooting, put his gun on the ground and become totally passive. I listened to fervent prayers of agreement all around me.

Then we heard the police cars racing into the entrances of our campus with their loud sirens wailing. Tires were screeching. Doors were slamming. Voices were yelling. Police cars kept pouring into the campus. We were praying.

Inexplicably, at that very moment, the gunman suddenly slumped down on the steps of the south entrance of the church and laid his gun down on the ground. Witnesses reported that he lay back against the doors and became lifeless. God had answered our prayers.

A policeman finally brought word to us that the gunman had been apprehended. There was a collective rush to the children. When I stepped out of the worship center, the scene was bizarre. Parents were consoling anxious children. People old and young were crying as the shock of the situation hit us. Police units were everywhere and more were arriving. Yellow tape was being strung around the property. The entire church campus had become a crime scene.

It was amazing how fast the satellite news vans pulled into the parking lot and started to extend their satellite dishes to broadcast our story around the nation. We were informed that no one could leave until the police sorted things out. We had experienced the power of God in an unplanned Sunday night prayer meeting.

I was pulled from the emotional scene when the police captain sought me out and told me that he needed me to give him a tour around our campus to survey the damage for his report. I walked the captain down our office wing when I heard him exclaim, "Huh, he missed him." I walked into the publications office and saw the source of his amusement. There was a bullet hole in a picture of Christ that hung on the wall. The bullet had missed the image of Christ's head by one inch. We later realized that our children, who had been moved to an inner room, were in the path of that very bullet. The bullet had gone through the picture and then through the wall before lodging in one-inch board that was centered in a wall of windows. Our children had been moved to the room on the other side of those windows. Had the bullet been the tiniest bit off, it would have hit in the middle of our children. We knew the picture of Christ was a sign to us. You had to go through him to get to our kids. Prayer works!

THE GREATEST MIRACLE

We were adding up the miracles. We had the miracle of the worship center and campus being shot up with no one killed or injured. Then we had the miracle of the one-inch board and the children being protected. We had yet to learn of the greatest miracle of the evening.

After the police interrogation, we learned the shocking truth. The gunman told the police that he had come that night to kill our children. His demonically twisted mind was convinced that he needed to send them home to Jesus before they reached the age of accountability and were hopelessly lost. Our families had been in far greater peril than any of us had imagined.

He had come to the church that evening after the service started and walked up to the gym doors intent on his gruesome mission. Our children's pastor noticed him standing there, through the windows in the gym doors. She later reported, "He just stood there looking strange." She recognized him because he had presented himself to her that morning as a dad who needed children's programming information. After a few moments she turned her attention back to the children who were laughing and playing a game that demanded her supervision.

Meanwhile, on the other side of the gym doors, the deranged man stood, gun in hand, staring in a murderous rage at our children.

When the police asked him why he did not go through those doors, he could not explain it. He said that he "kept trying to but something kept holding him back." Finally, in a fit of frustrated rage he had spun around and headed out of the gym on a wild shooting frenzy that completely circled our campus.

I have relived that night many times in my mind and heart. I remember, as if it were yesterday, the supernatural faith that God placed in our hearts as we prayed under fire. We had not realized that God, before we had even prayed, had already worked a great miracle for our children.

AUTHENTIC FAITH

There is one thing that you can be sure of in this fallen world. Sooner or later, trouble is coming your way. It may come on the highway, in the marketplace or even at church. We need to understand that these situations create the greatest opportunities for our personal growth. Peter, like everyone, learned the most from the things that he suffered. He wisely writes, "In this you greatly rejoice, even though now for a little while, if necessary, you have been distressed by various trials, so that the proof of your faith, being more precious than gold which is perishable, even though tested by fire, may be found to result in praise and glory and honor at the revelation of Jesus Christ" (1 Peter 1:6-7).

It is easy to say, "I have Faith." It is quite another to have had it tested in the fires of tribulation. The truth is that we need trouble in the neighborhood to help develop our character. Only when our Faith has been proven under fire can we truly celebrate its authenticity.

Faith is an inexplicable state of heart and mind that grants irrational peace in the midst of a hurricane of troubles. It is not primarily an intellectual understanding. We can know the facts that God is good and that he is on our side and still worry our self to death. It is more of a calming of our hearts. It is an inner knowing in our spirit that all is well.

Faith is completely unrelated to what we see in our circumstances. The eyes of Faith quiet us, for they apprehend a bigger view of life.

Our circumstances have not changed but Faith has changed us.

Faith destroys the emotional power of anxiety. Fear cannot sustain a credible influence in the presence of Faith. It is not that a Faith-filled person is unaware of a dire situation or will fail to take all available remedial actions. Faith does not cause a person to be out of touch with reality. It simply puts one's circumstantial reality in the context of a greater reality. It replaces primal fear with primal trust.

All this may sound like a lot of fanciful or mystical thinking to a person who has never experienced the gift of Faith. That reaction makes sense. Faith is an out-of-this-world experiential reality. Jesus made a promise: "My peace I give to you; not as the world gives do I give to you. Do not let your heart be troubled, nor let it be fearful" (John 14:27). I love the otherworldly irrationality of Faith!

Faith will never make sense to a rational person. It is something that you have to experience to understand. Once you do, you will never forget it. It is a life changer.

THE PROTECTION OF FAITH

Faith protects a person from nagging anxieties and all kinds of evil energies. The apostle Paul, who went through more than his share of dire predicaments, talked about how Faith can protect a person from malicious emotional attacks. "Above all, taking the shield of faith with which you will be able to quench all the fiery darts of the wicked one" (Ephesians 6:16 NKJV).

If you have lived very long you know all about fiery darts. They are like cruise missiles that wind their way through our defenses. They hit with a bang and start a fire. We can feed the fire into an inferno by nursing and rehearsing the unkind words that were spoken. We can let ourselves be blackened with bitterness. I like Paul's approach: pick up the shield of Faith. It is no wonder that he emphasizes "above all"—pick up that shield!

The manifestation of Faith, when we are under fire, is one of the greatest witnesses of the reality of Christ to an unbelieving world. People marvel at the peace and composure of a believer who is under duress. Disappointments are wrapped in peaceful trust. Faith gleams as the embers of God in the ash heap of our sorrows. Our deepest troubles are our greatest opportunities for Christ to grow and glow in us.

Paul encountered the mind-blowing impact of Faith in the midst of fiery troubles on more than one occasion. He writes about his experiences of Faith in a very enthusiastic way. "And the peace of God, which surpasses all comprehension, will guard your hearts and your minds in Christ Jesus" (Philippians 4:7). We, like Paul, need our hearts and minds to be protected from the incineration of worry and anxiety.

FAITH AND CHARACTER

God has a Faith agenda for you. You may not like it, but here it is. God is *more* concerned about what kind of person you are becoming than the difficult circumstances that you are going though in the moment. We often see things the other way around. Sometimes this puts us on a different page than God and leaves us frustrated. We want to live on Easy Street and God wants us to become combat veterans. We pray to be relieved of our distresses, and God prays for us to grow through them.

By the way, if you do not believe that God prays for you, then absorb this Bible revelation: "It is Christ who . . . is also risen, who is even at the right hand of God, who also makes intercession for us" (Romans 8:34 NKJV). Jesus does not just offer up an occasional prayer for us, but "He always lives to make intercession for them" (Hebrews 7:25). This is a thought worth pondering in the midst of our darkest moments.

Difficulties, if we respond properly, expand the quality of our character. Problems provide opportunities to encounter God's activity, which we would otherwise never experience. It takes a problem to discover God's faithfulness. The more we encounter God's faithfulness, the greater our capacity to trust him in the future. Greater trust creates a more balanced personality. It keeps us in the power zone.

James clearly believed this when he penned the following fanatical-sounding words: "Consider it all joy, my brethren, when you encounter various trials" (James 1:2). At first glance, his words sound like they came from a religious nutcase. A reasonable paraphrase of this verse is, "Be happy when you are bummed." Who in their right mind thinks like that? Eugene Peterson's paraphrase of this verse helps us to grasp the underlying reasoning: "Consider it a sheer gift, friends, when tests and challenges come at you from all sides. You know that under pressure, your faith-life is forced into the open and shows its true colors. So don't try to get out of anything prematurely. Let it do its work so you become mature and well-developed, not deficient in any way" (*The Message*).

Here is a good approach to life. When trouble comes, smile. You are about to need God. God is about to show himself faithful. You are going to grow in the quality of your character. Do not cut and run. Stand and believe. You will be stronger for it. Remember God's agenda. Get on his page and ditch yours.

THE POTENCY OF FAITH

Jesus said, "If you have faith the size of a mustard seed, you will say to this mountain, 'Move from here to there,' and it will move; and nothing will be impossible to you" (Matthew 17:20). A baseball-sized chunk of uranium-235 can explode with as much energy as 20,000 tons of TNT.[1] An explosion of that size resulted in a three-hundred-foot crater between eight and ten feet deep.[2] How powerful is Faith? A mustard seed is about one-tenth the size of a grain of rice, yet Faith can move entire mountains. Which is more potent? Do the math!

No known substance in the universe has the landscape-transforming power attributed to Faith. Faith does not just make a small crater in your problems. It moves entire mountains. A mustard seed! Really? What a message! No obstacle is too great for a person who has even a little bit of Faith. It is very potent stuff.

THE SYMPTOMS OF FAITH

Faith is a powerful, earth-moving, life-transforming force. It affects our hearts and minds in amazing ways. It fills us with confidence, boldness, courage and peace. Faith-filled people are highly motivated in very positive ways.

What is the alternative to Faith? Fear. This is not the motivational condition for beings made in the image of almighty God. Fear-based decisions are never in our best interests. Complete trust throws off the shackles of worry and empowers us to march through life with dignity. Faith happily produces a constant stream of good works. Paul understood this about Faith: "We remember before our God and Father your work produced by faith" (1 Thessalonians 1:3 NIV).

Faith-filled people have a very distinctive mix of character traits. Figure 7.1 highlights several of these from the Bible's inventory of Faith symptoms. When you put the character traits together, they paint an incredible mosaic of Faith. Faith thinks and feels differently. It believes and trusts. Faith-filled people act far differently than those who are filled with doubt and mistrust.

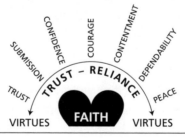

Figure 7.1

Pure Faith is fearless. It is convinced that God is fully in charge of the universe. It is not held hostage by the limitations of what is visible. "By faith we understand that the universe was formed at God's command, so that what is seen was not made out of what was visible" (Hebrews 11:3 NIV).

Faith knows that the unseen realm is where the seat of power resides. One command from God can change everything. That is w'

the apostle Paul did some pretty crazy, fearless stuff. He was motivated by invisible realities. He explained his actions with a very
simple phrase: "For we walk by faith, not by sight" (2 Corinthians 5:7).

Major outcomes of Faith are trust and submission. We have talked
about trust. Now let's turn our attention to the much-misunderstood
biblical concept of submission.

SUBMISSION

Submission is utterly contrary to human nature. Adam and Eve re-
belled against God, partly because they wanted to be like God.
Human nature still clamors for godhood on a very deep motivational
level. Gods don't submit.

I have had the privilege of raising six children. My favorite stage
is when they become teenagers. Teens have the intellectual capacity
of an adult and sometimes the emotional maturity of a child. One
daughter was such a good arguer that I finally said, "You do such a
good job making your case. Get a law degree and get paid for it."
Parents have the unenviable job of shaping little want-to-be-gods.

Submission boils down to a Faith issue. It circles back to our trust in
God. It may surprise you to learn that God commands us to adopt an
attitude of submission toward everyone. "Submit to one another out of
reverence for Christ" (Ephesians 5:21 NIV). Why is that? The key is
found in the word *reverence*. It means the kind of reverence and fear
that you would have for someone who has the power to hold you accountable. This is a message that speaks to both parties in a relationship.

The one in authority. Your character really stands out when you
are in charge. Leaders need to understand that they had better treat
people who are under their authority with respect. God is looking.
Faith m-¹   s careful about what we say and how we say it, knowing
             s after those who are powerless to help themselves. This
             ttention: "He who oppresses the poor taunts his Maker,
             gracious to the needy honors Him" (Proverbs 14:31).

Faith gives us the depth of perspective to be gracious in all our relationships, especially in leadership.

The one under authority. Your character can be severely tested when you are in a relationship where you are not the one in charge. How do you handle someone who abuses his or her authority? Faith answers a simple question: How big is your God? Is he bigger than the overbearing spouse or boss who aggravates you and begs a negative response? Can you trust God enough to submit to everyone, including an unfair person? If you really believe that God is in charge, the answer is simple: Yes you can! Trust God and you will ultimately prevail. Smile and remain confident in the purposes and plans that God has for you. Faith allows us to submit in peace regardless of our circumstances.

THE CONTINUUM OF FAITH

Faith, as was introduced in chapter four, can be perverted in one of two ways. The imbalances related to Faith are illustrated in figure 7.2. On the one hand, Faith can become diminished, making a person emotionally vulnerable to anxiety and, ultimately, the darkness of paralyzing fear.

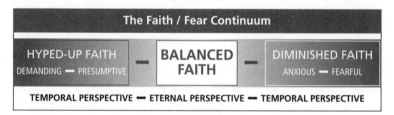

Figure 7.2

On the other hand Faith can be hyped up, overheated with false notions. Perhaps you have seen a very religious person who is hyped up on an extreme form of Faith, ordering God around like a butler. Presumptive pride resides at this address. This is a counterfeit of true Faith, which flourishes from the power of the Spirit in the power zone. True Faith is the humble and trusting middle between two extreme character imbalances.

FAITH HEALTH

Most people are moving so fast through life that they rarely stop long enough to think about the health of their Faith. The circumstances of life clamor for our full and immediate attention, often at the expense of self-awareness. We are wise to pause in the midst of doing life and ask, "How is my Faith?"

Personal assessments are the key to staying on track in the pursuit of your personal growth objectives. Take the free online assessment at SpiritualProgress.com for a detailed analysis of your strength and growth areas in Faith.

Personal reflection is much easier if we can picture ourselves through a simple visual model. Figure 7.3 provides such a model. It is a condensed biblical way of looking at the Faith aspect of one's character. It provides quick answers to important questions: Why am I acting this way? What are my greatest growth areas? What are my greatest strength areas? Figure 7.3 shows the full spectrum of character traits that are associated with Faith and the lack of it. The Motivational Virtue of Faith is positioned against the Motivational Evil of the lust of the flesh.

Figure 7.3

In the image of a divided heart, we see two primary motivational forces that are in opposition to one another. These opposing motivations produce very different personality traits and behaviors in people. One leads to submission and the other to manipulation. One is confident and secure while the other is insecure and possessive. One is at peace and contented while the other is anxious and unsatisfied. Faith does not walk by sight, but the lust of the eyes is all about what the eyes can see.

You might ask yourself, "Which kind of person would I prefer to hang out with?" Lust-of-the-eyes personality types tend to be "friends of convenience." Their needy quest may occupy their attention when you need them the most. Faith-filled people make life-long, loyal and supportive friends. Their trusting hearts make them highly trustworthy.

Faith and the lust of the eyes wage a deadly war. They battle to gain dominion over your heart. That is why Paul urged us to do what he had done: "Fight the good fight of faith" (1 Timothy 6:12) *for* "I have fought the good fight" (2 Timothy 4:7).

The lust of the eyes pulls you in the direction of your worldly desires. Faith expands your heart and allows you to rise above all the insecurities and dependencies of this world. Every day you make decisions that determine whether you end up feeding your Faith or feeding your lusts. God will never overstep your free will. The motivation that you feed the most is the one that wins the most.

FINAL THOUGHTS

The lust of the eyes is always in a "wanting" condition. Shopping binges are but a temporary distraction for this voracious lust. Why do we have such a compelling need for things? What is the source of the underlying anxiety that drives us to overspend and get in debt?

The lust of the eyes feeds on our insecurities. This lust lures us into a vain search for significance in a universe that appears, to the uninformed, to offer few other options. Possessing some new "thing" creates a momentary, feel-good escape. For many, the accumulation of wealth or beautiful things becomes a lifelong quest to create and sustain a sense of personal significance.

Why is there such a persistent longing for greater significance in the human heart? The answer is simple. In the beginning, God created Adam and Eve as great and glorious creatures of perfection and beauty. All humanity presently abides in a far lesser state than God's original design. The human spirit longs for the greatness from which it has fallen. Paul noted, "For all have sinned and fall short of the glory of God" (Romans 3:23). How can such a void be filled? Faith is a big part of the answer.

Faith-filled people live in an "abundance" condition. They are not bound up with the need to consume or acquire resources to feel better about themselves. Faith assures a person of their inestimable value to God. How valuable are you? God made a statement about your significance that is pretty amazing. "For God so loved the world [you], that He gave His only begotten Son, that whoever believes in Him shall not perish, but have eternal life" (John 3:16).

You are of inestimable significance to God. He took on the form of man to pursue you. He gave himself for you. God believes in your worth, and God is always right. Faith sees what God believes.

Embrace the Motivational Virtue of Faith. Walk in the Spirit, read the Word and embrace community. Put yourself in a place where God can speak to you about your level of Faith. Discover the spiritual disciplines that best work for you. God wants you to grow in Faith, so grow in Faith! It will define your character and change everything about your life.

8

THE DISTORTIONS OF FAITH

Faith Imbalances and the Power Zone

> *All I have seen teaches me to trust the*
> *Creator for all I have not seen.*
>
> Ralph Waldo Emerson

> *For by grace you have been saved through faith;*
> *and that not of yourselves, it is the gift of God.*
>
> Ephesians 2:8

Before we dig into the imbalances of Faith, let's take another good look at the real thing. There are many aberrations of true Faith. The more you know the genuine article, the easier it is to spot a counterfeit.

REAL FAITH

Faith, as a Motivational Virtue, inspires us to completely trust in God. It goads us until we fully submit our life and will to his purposes. True Faith does not tolerate addictions to worry or anxious labors to fix an unfixable problem. Faith means that you have turned the steering wheel of your life over to God.

Imagine your Faith under severe assault. The emotional onslaught of fear threatens to engulf you. Catastrophes lurk in the dark corners of your mind. Panic is about to win out and define your character. Then you remember, *I have been here before*. In fact, you have been there many times before. Each and every time, Faith was overrun with fear. You have tried your way long enough, and worry has never gotten you anywhere. This time you have been preparing. You have been immersed in God's Word and the Spirit. You are part of a spiritual support circle. Faith in the goodness and power of God has blossomed. You are facing a God-sized problem. This time you are finally going to rely on God.

God is there. He has been waiting for this moment. He meets you at the corner of Trust and Surrender Boulevards. He embraces you as you embrace him. He imparts *his gift of Faith*. Your believing takes on deeper dimensions. The Spirit ministers to your spirit. You are engaged in a miraculous character-building partnership. Your motivational core is shifting. The adventure has begun—a lifetime of trust!

CHARACTER TRANSFORMATION

The gift of Faith has an immeasurable impact on a person's character. It affects every area of your life. Faith produces, among other things, the distinctive character trait of peacefulness. Contrast this with the people you know who are anxious and restless.

Jesus is called the "Lord of Peace." I love Paul's prayer: "May the Lord of peace Himself continually grant you peace in every circumstance" (2 Thessalonians 3:16). Peace changes a person's countenance. Gone is the angst of looming catastrophes and the frustration of feeling like the world is against you.

Peace has adopted a new attitude toward life. "If God is for us, who is against us?" (Romans 8:31). The Master of the universe is now in your corner. You have a smile on your face and a bounce in your step. Your circumstances have not changed, but Faith has changed you. People around you cannot help but notice the difference. You have become a real-time barometer of the reality of an invisible God.

Your Faith will be tested. Call it character development. Things may get worse before they get better. Honestly, in spite of what some people say, things on this earth may not change for the better. This does not weaken the foundation of Faith. God is on your side! He is committed to the best and greatest outcomes for your life. He sees the big picture of your eternal future and he *will* bring it to pass. Faith transforms an anxiety-ridden personality into a calm, trusting soul.

THE EYES OF FAITH

It is the way of this world that circumstances often hide the truth. God *could* constantly intervene in our circumstances. He *could* make your life easy and reveal his goodness like an on-demand movie. You would not need Faith were he to fix every problem.

But Faith is for us. We need it. Troubles force us to deal with our headstrong, insecure natures. They bring us back, again and again, to the same fork in the road. Will we go our willful way or the way of Faith? How will we relate to God—best friend or uncaring acquaintance?

The life of Faith is a life of surrender. We start out learning how to surrender small things. Faith in full bloom peacefully accepts the loss of all things. I have stood by the deathbeds of Faith-filled people and observed the miracle of Faith. In the worst of times, Faith still *knows* that God has not taken a vacation. He is ceaselessly and actively monitoring everything about us down to amazing details. Jesus said, "The very hairs of your head are all numbered" (Matthew 10:30).

He is personally engaged in our welfare. "And we know that God causes all things to work together for good to those who love God, to those who are called according to His purpose" (Romans 8:28). I love the words *and we know*. Faith is a kind of knowing. It is not an intelligence that the world can understand. It is more like having street smarts about God. It is spiritual intelligence.

Walking by Faith is the road less traveled, but don't be mistaken, you are not alone. Multitudes have gone before you. The apostle Paul walked this way. He pointed the way for others with the words, "For we walk by faith, not by sight" (2 Corinthians 5:7). Paul marched through many great dangers right up until the day he fearlessly faced his own death. Faith wants to walk that far with you. When your body begins to deteriorate with age, Faith can more than compensate for it by invigorating your eternal spirit. "Therefore we do not lose heart, but though our outer man is decaying, yet our inner man is being renewed day by day" (2 Corinthians 4:16). This is the motivational power of Faith.

THE CONTAGION OF FAITH

I love being around elderly people who have grown in genuine Faith until they are literally bursting with it. A number of years ago I hired such a man to join our pastoral staff part time. He had retired from a long and fruitful career as a pastor. He conducted a powerful devotional every week in our pastoral staff meetings. Every time he opened God's Word and began to discuss spiritual realities, he was transformed. His face glowed, his voice captivated us and his blue eyes shone brightly. Every week, he transformed into an ageless being right in front of us. His eyes of Faith gifted us on many occasions with a piercing glimpse into eternity. He lived the words of 2 Corinthians 4:18: "We look not at the things which are seen, but at the things which are not seen; for the things which are seen are temporal, but the things which are not seen are eternal." Pastor Andy Slack personified the first character profile of Faith that is illustrated below. I envision him doing a dance in heaven ever since his passing into the arms of Jesus.

CHARACTER PROFILE OF FAITH NUMBER ONE:
The Peaceful Persona

Figure 8.1 illustrates a person who has grown into a mature and

balanced Faith. They are not struggling with their feelings about
God's goodness. They have come
to trust in his commitment to their
highest good. They trust enough to

Discover your "Faith intelligence" by taking the free assessment at SpiritualProgress.com.

believe that God will take care of the difficult circumstances and
the obnoxious people in their lives. Their character can be summarized as "peaceful in the midst of the storm." Balanced Faith
people are a shining light in a fear-filled world. They have the
strength of character to rise above the motivational fears that
cause others to run about in disarray.

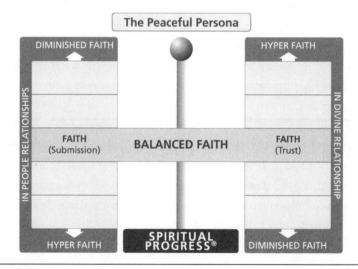

Figure 8.1

In the balance figures of this chapter, you may notice a correlation
between divine and human relationships. The two cannot be sepa-
rated. How well you relate to God has a direct impact on how well
you relate to your spouse, children, friends and acquaintances. The
association is so strong that it is possible to assess a person's Faith in

God from the way they relate to people. This is helpful because one's relationship with God can be largely invisible. A person's relationships with people are highly visible. It is impossible for a person to claim that they have great Faith in God when they have anxiety-ridden relationships. The correlation between how we relate to God and people will become even clearer as we walk through the four imbalanced character profiles of faith below.

The gray bar in the center of figure 8.1 illustrates balanced Faith. The right side pictures a person who has a Faith (trust) relationship with God. The left side shows an associated Faith (submission) relationship with people. The two represent the harmonious balance of genuine Faith.

Why typify Faith on the human-relations side as submission? Submission penetrates, on a deep motivational level, to the way we relate with people. Are we at rest, or are we trying to control the people in our lives? Manipulation and mutiny are not the way of Faith. Nor are isolation and anxiety.

Those who have a mature, God-centered view of the universe know that personal control over our circumstances is largely an illusion. Yet there are some things in life we can control. Submission, for example, is a matter of taking positive control of a relationship, whereas rebellion lets a negative relationship control you. Jesus gave some life-changing advice to the Jews of his day.

Roman soldiers could conscript any citizen to carry a load for one mile. The Jews resented being pack mules for the Romans, but Jesus taught something extraordinary. "Whoever forces you to go one mile, go with him two" (Matthew 5:41). Why? The second mile expresses your free will. You have taken control. Interesting conversations can even occur during the second mile. It's life-changing turf.

It is easy to say, "I have Faith in God," but talk is cheap. God is invisible. People are in your face. We all possess an uncanny ability to deceive ourselves and to rate ourselves more highly than others view us. It is helpful to know that the Bible describes the symptoms of Faith in terms that are easily seen and verifiable by others. This makes it possible for others to accurately assess the character of our Faith.

The way we treat people validates the authenticity of our Faith. It is fair to ask, "If you have so much Faith in God, why are you fighting so much with your spouse?" Is your marriage something that God cannot handle? Lay down your sword. Quit arguing. Walk the second mile! Walk in Faith! Watch God work on your behalf. Obnoxious and difficult relationships are a gift to us. They purify our Faith. They deliver us from being a religious actor.

The ability to submit to the difficult people that God has placed in your life is an honest measure of your Faith in God. Is God bigger than your boss? Who's in control of your world? Only people who profoundly trust in God have the depth of character to genuinely and confidently submit to difficult people.

Of course, there is a rare but clear exception to this prescription for submitting to others by Faith. *No one* has the right to force compliance to anything that violates the moral laws of God. Submission to people must always remain within the larger context of submission to God. The words of Peter come to mind: "We must obey God rather than men" (Acts 5:29).

CHARACTER PROFILE OF FAITH NUMBER TWO:
The Guarded Persona

Figure 8.2 is the first profile of imbalanced Faith. It illustrates what happens when our Faith in God is diminished. Lessened Faith impacts the way we relate to God and to people. Left untreated, the guarded persona (somewhat diminished Faith) will take on more of the extreme personality traits of the suffering persona (greatly diminished Faith), which is described in the next section.

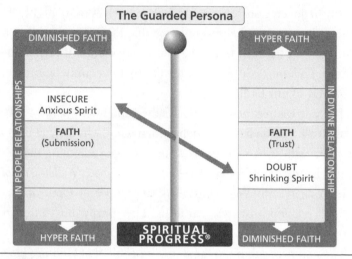

Figure 8.2

Relating to God. Diminished Faith means that you have a lessened confidence that God is on your side. An increased degree of separation from God produces predictable results. Absence does not make the heart grow fonder; absence makes the heart grow more fearful. Faith is displaced by doubt. Confidence in God's goodness is undermined.

Perhaps you have been so busy and preoccupied that you have not taken the time to invest in your spiritual life. Maybe you have gone through a bad experience where you feel like God let you down. Instead of doing the spiritual work to resolve your feelings, you left matters on hold. These are ways in which confidence in God's goodness becomes undermined. Without God at your back, the anxious mind sees potential dangers lurking in every corner. The impact of anxiety on your relationships with people is far-reaching.

Relating to people. Diminished Faith in God increases our vulnerability to evil. We develop a distorted view of reality. Fear is powered by an amplified belief in the power of people to harm us.

Anxiety is a primary symptom of someone who has a Faith problem. Diminished Faith robs us of personal confidence. We no longer bask in the perceived security of God's favor. We feel more alone. If we cannot trust God, then we certainly cannot trust people.

We become guarded. This leads to an increased degree of separation from people, which produces predictable results. Our insecurities undermine our capacity to be openly transparent with people. Guardedness makes it easy for others to misread us. We appear distant and aloof. People may think of us as selfish or arrogant. They become guarded toward us. This starts a cycle of dysfunctional mistrust. When we perceive others as emotionally withdrawn from us, it serves to confirm our worst suspicions. The fear-laden dance of mistrust goes on and on.

The destructive power of fear is one reason why Jesus strongly rebuked a lack of Faith whenever he saw it in the lives of his disciples. He wanted more for his followers. Jesus aspires for his children to have open, trusting, fearless relationships with God and people. Faith has a huge impact on the caliber of your relationships and therefore, the quality of your life.

Faith-filled people do experience problems. They just live above the hurricanes of anxiety that swirl about them. Diminished Faith is one of the chief reasons our world is so socially isolated. God is working to put the world back together again, one relationship at a time. He wants to fill you with Faith and your life with positive, supportive relationships.

What's your path to greater Faith? Fill your mind with more positive messages than negative ones. Faith grows from regular exposure to the Bible. "Faith comes from hearing, and hearing by the word of Christ" (Romans 10:17). When it comes to

Growth plans found at SpiritualProgress.com are designed as bite-sized daily devotionals. They are delivered to your mobile device to sustain an uninterrupted flow of God's Word into your life, wherever you are.

the Bible, frequency and consistency are more important to our spiritual health than infrequent large doses.

CHARACTER PROFILE OF FAITH NUMBER THREE:
The Suffering Persona

The suffering persona illustrates what happens when Faith becomes severely diminished. As the word *suffering* implies, this is a very un-comfortable place for the soul. Diminished Faith is a progressive dis-ease of character. It begins when we entertain anxieties, and ends up with anxieties controlling us.

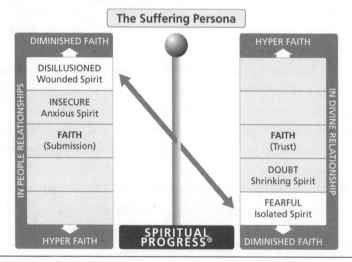

Figure 8.3

Low-Faith people have put themselves in harm's way. They not only have to deal with the real problems of life, but they must also contend with every possible evil scenario that *might* happen. Worst-case scenarios torment the mind. We worry as if it might actually make a difference. Jesus taught, "And who of you by being worried can add a single hour to his life?" (Matthew 6:27).

Faith presents us with a deciding point in the path of life. Will we

learn to trust and abide in the arms of a ferociously l[
Bible describes the blessings of this character conditi[

> Blessed is the man who trusts in the LORD
> And whose trust is the LORD. For he will be like a tree planted
>   by the water,
> That extends its roots by a stream
> And will not fear when the heat comes;
> But its leaves will be green,
> And it will not be anxious in a year of drought
> Nor cease to yield fruit. (Jeremiah 17:7-8)

Faith living is confident living. Heat always comes! But Faith keeps bearing fruit.

Another deciding point is the more heavily traveled path. Leave behind the pastoral imagery of trees and flowing water, and picture yourself heading into a huge, hot, desolate desert. The Bible describes the end of the road for those who lose all Faith.

> Cursed is the man who trusts in mankind
> And makes flesh his strength,
> And whose heart turns away from the LORD.
> For he will be like a bush in the desert
> And will not see when prosperity comes,
> But will live in stony wastes in the wilderness,
> A land of salt without inhabitant. (Jeremiah 17:5-6)

This is a curse of our own making. Faith-filled people are filled with truth and walk in the assurance of God's care and provision. Low-Faith people walk in varying measures of spiritual darkness. This is no condition in which to navigate life. The driver always ends up in the ditch. This is why Faith and the matter of growing in Faith is such a big deal to God.

The motivating power of fear. Fear, like all lusts, is something that can become a runaway train. Fear is a self-feeding, self-defeating and self-destructive machine. We have large samplings of data that prove this to be true. Just look at what happens to the stock market when fear moves in. It starts a stampede. Fear begets fear. Winston Churchill understood this. At a time when fear threatened to engulf England, he uttered some of his truest words: "The only thing we have to fear is fear itself."

Relating to God. God is our most primal relationship. Our psyches were created to operate in the confidence of his presence. His absence makes us vulnerable and apprehensive. Low-Faith people have a diminished perception of God's protective care. The void makes them insecure, which makes for a restless, unhappy personality.

Suffering personas have become largely isolated from God. This is an advanced stage of doubt. They warily stare at God (if they look at all) across a chasm of mistrust and anger. Resentment assassinates God's character. "God has let me down. He has not come through for me. I am a victim of divine neglect." This negative view of your heavenly Father has a profound effect on how you relate to other people.

Relating to people. Confident, Faith-filled people have an assured view about life. Their affirmative energy attracts people like moths to a light. They have lots of friends.

Untrusting people have the opposite effect on others. Low Faith sees a very different world through a heightened sense that people are against us. This persona may develop a martyr complex: "I am the victim of an unloving world." This leads to suffering personalities who lug their wounded heart from relationship to relationship and church to church. The good news is that people with a suffering persona can grow into a person of great Faith. Faith highway is filled with miraculous comeback stories.

Diminished faith and divorce. John and Mary were like many couples today. Mary had been through five divorces and John one. They had wed with the greatest of hopes. Smiley faces disappeared a scant five months later. John asked me to meet him for coffee. "Pastor," he anguished, "she has been through many divorces before. She knows what she is doing. She has an attorney, and she is going to take my business and destroy my life."

"John," I began, "you must be a pretty arrogant guy." He looked shocked at my apparent off-subject remark.

"What are you talking about?" he asked incredulously.

I pressed forward. "Susan had been married five times before you married her. You must have thought that you were a much better man than all the previous men. Surely you knew it would take an extraordinary effort on your part to make this marriage work. By marrying her you were declaring to the world that you were willing to walk where five other men could not."

The words began to impact him. For the first time in weeks, he took his eyes off of being the victim and put them on to the issue of his character.

I continued, "The only question here is if you have enough Faith in God to walk where no one has walked. If you are going to trust him unconditionally, then you are going to have to unconditionally love her."

He lowered his head in recognition of the truth. I went on, "This is a Faith issue. It is your opportunity to become a man of Faith. You can get an attorney and fight her, or you can take the other fork in the road. If you choose Faith, God will be there to walk the journey with you. You are going to have to do something radically different than the other five men did if you are to succeed where they did not."

We prayed and John went off to meet with his wife. His Faith had been rekindled. Hours later I got a call from John. He was utterly amazed at how things had turned around once he stepped out in Faith. Love was restored. Faith had broken the power of mutual fear and distrust. I am happy to report that after many years, they remain a happily married couple.

CHARACTER PROFILE OF FAITH NUMBER FOUR:
The Controlling Persona

Figure 8.4 illustrates the relational impact when an imbalance of Faith heads in the opposite direction from fear. Hyper Faith is a presumptuous, widespread spiritual imbalance that usually comes from the hearts of highly enthused people who have an incomplete understanding of the Bible.

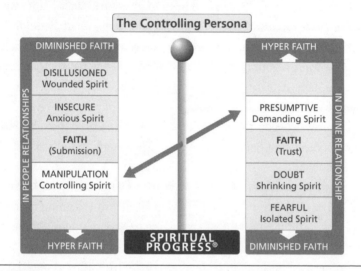

Figure 8.4

Healthy character development, as we've seen, requires a balance between diminished Faith and hyper Faith. Hyper Faith, in spite of its strong Faith-like appearance, is imbalanced Faith. How can you discern the difference between hyper Faith and true Faith? The answer is simple. Examine the caliber of a person's relationships. Let's first look at the God side.

Relating to God. People headed in the direction of hyper Faith begin to talk to God differently. Why? Presumption! Prayer requests shift away from the context of an intimate, trusting conversation with a friend to one of making authoritative petitions. That's a step backwards. Instead of sharing their heart *with* God they start talking *at* God. Hyper Faith prayers often incorporate language that sounds like a legal argument. They line up a list of Bible promises like a well-reasoned case. It almost seems as if they feel a need to hold God accountable to his Word. Really? Does God need convincing to be true to his Word? Who are they trying to convince?

There is nothing wrong with quoting God's promises when we pray, but it is important to realize that they are for us, not God. Quoting Scriptures does not put God under additional obligation. No amount of praying could increase his Love and commitment to our welfare. He wants to bless us! God's promises help us to understand how seriously God takes us when we pray in Faith. They teach us to pray with a sense of expectation and confidence. They build our Faith.

Here is a Faith-building idea. Instead of listing God's promises every time you pray, why not try bragging on his character? Talk about his goodness and faithfulness. Talk about his Love and commitment to our highest good. "Enter His gates with thanksgiving and His courts with praise. Give thanks to Him, bless His name" (Psalm 100:4). Worshipful praying always carries with it the appropriate tone of trust, which is the essence of Faith!

Let's get to the heart of the error of hyped Faith. *Every* promise in the Bible has to be understood within the context of God's sovereignty. God is smarter than us. It is never wise to think that we can trump his will with our Faith. God sees the big picture in *every* circumstance. "For as the heavens are higher than the earth, so are My ways higher than your ways and My thoughts than your thoughts" (Isaiah 55:9). God's will is *always* the best-desired outcome. I thank God, in hindsight, that he did not answer some of my most passionate prayers over the years. In many cases I would have gotten second best or worse!

Many people think that Faith is primarily about how you pray—"I need to pray, so it is time to put on my Faith mantle." But praying is a small part of living a life of Faith. Faith is not just for prayer time; it is for all the time. People of Faith walk by Faith, give by Faith, work by Faith and naturally pray by Faith.

Effective praying. God has invited us into his intimate counsel chambers. I love Jesus' perspective: "I have called you friends, for all things that I have heard from My Father I have made known to you" (John 15:15). Prayer should be a comfortable, friendly place.

God is moved by Faith, never by well-worded arguments or manipulation. Trust is what earned Abraham the moniker "The Father of Faith" (Romans 4:16). He raised the knife over his only son in a radical act of surrender to God. His amazing Faith story is recorded in Genesis 22:1-18.

It is a big step backwards to try and force the hand of an omnipotent God through the power of reason. Volumes could be written on the subject of prayer, but this one principle is the gist of much of it: God looks at the condition of our hearts when we pray and not the content of our words.

Jesus taught us how to pray. We begin by realigning our hearts with him and his purposes: "Your kingdom come; Your will be done, on earth as it is in heaven" (Matthew 6:10). It is only after our hearts have been rightly aligned with God that we are spiritually prepared to share our needs with God. "Give us this day our daily bread" (Matthew 6:11).

The Lord's Prayer is the only place in the Bible where Jesus gave detailed instructions on *how* to relate to our heavenly Father in prayer. How then do Christian people get their manner of praying all messed up? They take "claiming the promises of God" as a license to go another way.

Let me speak for a moment to those who have been exposed to and participated in hyper-Faith praying. You may feel that something that is sacred to you is under attack. This is not the case. You can relationally pray and still be very passionate in how you pray. But there is one big difference with relational praying. Your confidence is not based on a promise, which may not apply to your situation. Instead your confidence is secure in the absolute goodness of his character. Relational praying is all about love and trust.

The one thing you can be certain of is God's commitment to your highest good. You can boldly intercede and trust in his promises without presuming how God *must* act in a given situation. Remember the bottom line—"Your will be done." Press in to an intimacy with God and discover the real power of praying in Faith.

Balanced praying. King David of ancient Israel knew how to pray. God called him "a man after my heart, who will do all my will" (Acts 13:22). There is a pungent story about David's prayer life that perfectly illustrates how to balance passion and submission.

David had a big heart for God, but he blew it bigtime. His sin with Bathsheba reached headline status in the nation. The child that had been conceived through his sin was dying. David stopped eating and started praying. He lay on the ground for seven days and cried out to God to spare his child. When the child died, his palace staff panicked. What would David do now? When David heard the bad news, he got up, took a shower, worshiped and sat down to eat. He explained his behavior when confused onlookers questioned him: "'While the child was alive, you fasted and wept; but when the child died, you arose and ate food.' He said, 'While the child was still alive, I fasted and wept; for I said, "Who knows, the LORD may be gracious to me, that the child may live." But now he has died; why should I fast? Can I bring him back again?'" (2 Samuel 12:21-23). Pray with passion and trust God with the results. That is balanced praying.

Relating to people. When a person takes the ego posture of "I know best," how do you think they will treat the people around them? Hyper-Faith people typically have poor boundaries. This can get way out of control with hyper-Faith pastors. They overreach in their people relationships in the same way they overreach in the way they relate to God. If they know what is best for God, why shouldn't they know what is best for you?

Hyper-Faith people often act like they have an operator's license to help God accomplish his will. Perhaps God will be too busy to notice my or your situation until it is too late. This raises the honest question: "How engaged is God in the details of your daily life?" The answer that Jesus gives may surprise you! "The very hairs of your head are all numbered" (Matthew 10:30). That is a scope of divine awareness and engagement that boggles the mind. Faith rests in the peace of knowing God's amazing attentiveness to our highest welfare. The good news is that people with a controlling persona can grow into people of better balanced Faith.

When you live in the dorms of a Christian college, some weird things can happen. Susie was a good friend and a classmate of mine. She pulled me aside one day to share an unpleasant dilemma. I was amused to hear that three different students had recently approached Susie with the news, "God has told me that you are to be my wife." I knew all three of the guys. We sat down and discussed the possibilities. Either God was confused, or he kept changing his mind, or something else was afoot.

"The way I see it," I said, "is that God operates on a need-to-know basis. If you are to be the wife of someone, *you* are on the 'need-to-know' list and he will personally tell you." I have used that principle in innumerable situations through many years of ministry. In the ensuing decades, I have also seen countless forms of relational manipulation, spiritualized under the heading, "God told me."

CHARACTER PROFILE OF FAITH NUMBER FIVE:
The Domineering Persona

The domineering persona is the picture of what happens when one's Faith has become more severely hyped up. Hyper Faith impacts the way we relate to God and to people. Left untreated, the controlling persona (somewhat hyped Faith) has taken on more of the extreme personality traits of the domineering persona (highly hyped Faith). Personas of this nature have migrated from presumption to a deep-rooted sense of entitlement. Whether or not they know it, they have begun to take on the prerogatives of a god.

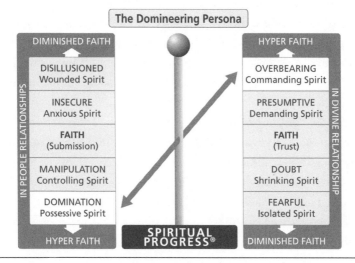

Figure 8.5

Extreme hyper Faith. In some cases you have to see it to believe how far extreme-hyper-Faith individuals can go. I recall being in a meeting many years ago when the speaker made a God-like pronouncement. "Everyone who gives $5,000 in the next fifteen minutes will never be sick a day of their life." That's the most affordable health care plan I have ever heard about! The problem is that it was presumption and not Faith. I am not sure if the speaker actually believed what he was saying or if he was a charlatan. Both are possible.

Many of these extreme-hyper-Faith individuals have the surprising ability to gain large followings. Their charisma and overconfidence is perceived as profound evidence of Faith by the undiscerning masses. They casually rebuke demonic entities, mock the devil, and

are filled with an endless sense of self-importance. It reminds me of
the character flaws that Peter condemned in the false prophets of his
day, "those who . . . despise authority. Daring, self-willed, they do not
tremble when they revile angelic majesties" (2 Peter 2:10). Peter, who
was taken aback at their level of pride, continued his rant: "Angels
who are greater in might and power do not bring a reviling judgment
against them before the Lord. But these, like unreasoning animals,
born as creatures of instinct to be captured and killed, reviling where
they have no knowledge, will in the destruction of those creatures
also be destroyed" (2 Peter 2:11-12). I can't imagine Peter using stronger
words to confront a domineering persona.

Tendencies and traits. The extreme pride of the domineering
persona makes individuals with this affliction very difficult to reach.
You don't touch the Lord's anointed! They have adopted a belief
system that is highly defended. Their "belief" is false Faith. Pride has
matured into the darkness of evil arrogance.

I have observed a number of tendencies over the years associated
with people who possess this extreme spiritual imbalance.

1. They have a tendency to overemphasize money and the accumulation of wealth. False Faith becomes focused on things.

2. They have the tendency to build a personal kingdom. They do
   not cooperate well with those who are not under their sway. They
   tend to be territorial and highly possessive of people, especially
   those who give them money.

3. Their lack of boundaries with people can also lead to sexual immorality; all the while they advertise extreme religious fervor.

These hyped-up individuals represent yet another case where
spiritual fervor collapses under the weight of a severe character imbalance. This kind of religious extremism has done immeasurable
damage to the church and to the people they control. Sometimes it
takes a hard-hitting diagnosis before people become motivated

enough to change. An accurate spiritual assessment, such as the one available at SpiritualProgress.com, will be beneficial. Nevertheless, no matter a person's assessment results, with God everyone can grow.

FINAL THOUGHTS

In this chapter I have spent a good deal of time confronting hyper Faith. I realize some readers may be questioning my level of Faith in miracles. I can assure you that I have prayed for and seen many amazing miracles in my twenty-five-plus years of being a pastor. I close out this chapter by sharing two great Faith stories that are precious to me.

Albert and the angel. Albert had been a man of prayer for as long as anyone could remember. He was a pillar in the church, but was now on his deathbed. I was standing with a group of praying men who encircled his hospital bed while death approached. We were holding hands when an individual whom we assumed was a hospital orderly joined our circle. Suddenly a beautiful smile crossed Albert's face. He raised his hands heavenward and exhaled the name of Jesus with his last breath. We were awestruck with his incredible passage into the loving arms of Christ. The orderly hurried out of the room, and Albert's brother followed him to thank him for his prayers. As he entered the hallway the orderly was simply not there. He had vanished almost before his eyes. In the worshipful moments that followed, we all concluded that an angel had joined us at the moment of Albert's passing.

Victorious Beverly. Beverly was a chronic worrier. I should add that she was one of the most loving and considerate people I have ever known. Like many Christians she suffered the spiritual imbalance of being strong in Love and weak in Faith. She burdened her family with her constant fears and predictions of disaster. Then one day she was diagnosed with late-stage terminal cancer. When I received word of the diagnosis, I was both saddened and deeply concerned with how she would process such news. What I witnessed over the five weeks leading up to her death was nothing less than amazing. In the midst of her greatest crisis, she finally apprehended the bigness and goodness of her God. Where her life had been typified by constant anxiety, her last days were characterized by an ever-present smile on her face. Her personal transformation was a profound witness to her family and others. Sadly, it took a tragedy for her to throw down her fears and discover the unfathomable peace of Christ.

Albert and Beverly remind me of the power of true Faith. There are times when we need to travail, cry out to God and pray without ceasing. There is nothing that is too difficult for God. I have seen and I believe in miracles! I simply cannot believe that I should or could manipulate God's will to meet my needs. I have too much Faith in his goodness and wisdom to ever want to violate his will. His will be done!

9

HOPE

The Optimism Virtue

> *The pessimist sees difficulty in every opportunity.*
> *The optimist sees the opportunity in every difficulty.*
>
> Winston Churchill

> *Looking for the blessed hope*
> *and the appearing of the glory of our*
> *great God and Savior, Christ Jesus.*
>
> Titus 2:13

There are many things that can consume our attention. Life can get so hectic that we run from one distraction to another. But if you are a Christian, you cannot afford to lose sight of Hope for very long. It celebrates the biggest reality of your life. Without Hope you lose your shine. Your motivations succumb to the negative messages of this world. Diminished Hope leads to silence instead of cheering.

The apostles, right after Jesus ascended to heaven, showcased Hope in their message: "And with great power the apostles were giving testimony to the resurrection of the Lord Jesus, and abundant grace was upon them all" (Acts 4:33). Eternal life is still headline news.

We need to keep the main thing the main thing. The apostle John, toward the end of his life, recalled the personal promise that Jesus made to him and the other disciples: "This is the promise which He Himself made to us: eternal life" (1 John 2:25). Hope never stopped being a really big deal to John.

Paul introduced his ministry in terms of his Hope. "Paul . . . in the hope of eternal life, which God, who cannot lie, promised long ages ago" (Titus 1:1-2). We need to think of ourselves in terms of Hope. It changes things when we operate in the reality that "I am an eternal being!" It transforms our behaviors.

THE CELEBRATION DANCE

Faith opens the door to the spiritual life. Hope is the joyful dance that begins just inside the door. Hope, at its core, is celebratory. Paul puts it this way: "We have obtained our introduction by faith into this grace in which we stand; and we exult in hope of the glory of God" (Romans 5:2). I, for one, want to move beyond the introductory stage of the spiritual life. I want to exult and dance in joyful celebration of the victory that Christ has wrought on my behalf! It is the greatest triumph ever accomplished!

Given the amazing magnitude of the victory, it makes one wonder. Where are the noisy cheering fans? Why aren't there multitudes of stomping feet, clapping hands and shouts of triumphant joy from the people of God? Why are believers so largely silent and reserved? It's like the crowd is distracted and has taken their eyes off the field of victory.

CONSIDER THE FINAL SCORE
Immortality 1, Death 0

Look at Paul's jubilant recap of the game. He excitedly taunts the defeated foe. The word *victory* is enthusiastically mentioned three times in quick succession. Rah!

But when this perishable will have put on the imperishable, and this mortal will have put on immortality, then will come about the saying that is written, "Death is swallowed up in victory. O death, where is your victory? O death, where is your sting?" The sting of death is sin, and the power of sin is the law; but thanks be to God, who gives us the victory through our Lord Jesus Christ. (1 Corinthians 15:54-57)

It's shocking that more of God's children aren't passionately celebrating *their* victory. Eternal life is the astounding, amazing, phenomenal win for every believer. It is the victory that makes every other issue shrink to insignificance. Karl Marx mistakenly called this approach to religion "the opiate of the masses." Biblical Hope does not lull us asleep, while wait for the by and by. It gives us the boldness and confidence to more fully engage and transform the world in the face of every obstacle.

- Got an abusive boss? Will that be a big deal to you in 100,000 years?

- Struggling with sorrows? God will wipe every tear from your eyes (Revelation 7:17).

- Got a financial crisis? You will spend eternity walking on streets of gold (Revelation 21:21).

- Is your body dying? You get to trade it in for a new imperishable body (1 Corinthians 15:42).

What reasonable effect should Hope have on my life? Paul explains the impact of this win: "Therefore, my beloved brethren, be steadfast, immovable, always abounding in the work of the Lord, knowing that your toil is not in vain in the Lord" (1 Corinthians 15:58). Hope empowers me to *never* quit!

THE EFFECT OF HOPE

Hope, for a Christian, means that you are a winner. Don't you think it is time you acted like it? Hope defines us. Every day when we walk out the door, we head into a lost world. People desperately need to see the light of Hope.

The war is over. Everything is complete but the awards ceremony. Hope makes us undefeatable for we have already won. It gives us toughness and resilience in the face of daunting obstacles and ugly circumstances. Hope makes us laugh at the promises and the threats of this world. What can you offer me that compares to eternal life? What threat can you terrorize me with now that death has been defeated?

Hope gives us the disposition of a traveler, passing through. This world is only prepping me for my eternal destiny. We seek a better country (Hebrews 11:16).

Hope makes us happy. This is not the temporary laughter of fleeting pleasure, but the soul-jostling joy that smiles in the face of adversity (Romans 15:13). We grin in anticipation.

A HOPE CRISIS

Think of the collective witness that millions upon millions of Christians filled with Hope would make in our low-Hope world. The jubilant shout would be deafening. It would restore pungency to the gospel and authenticity to the church. We need a revival of the virtue of Hope.

What's up with this relative silence? It makes one wonder if Christ's followers really believe what they say they believe. The church needs to create more Hope-filled believers.

I came to know Christ as my personal friend on February 11, 1971. It was during the height of what has been called the Jesus Movement. As a teenager and spiritual infant, I was steered to Calvary Chapel Costa Mesa with Pastor Chuck Smith. I recall one thing above all else from those exciting days as a young believer: I was nurtured in a strong sense of Hope under pastor Chuck's teaching.

We were all "looking for the blessed hope and the appearing of the glory of our great God and Savior, Christ Jesus" (Titus 2:13). Every day I wondered, "Is this the day Jesus will come back?" It spiritually energized every aspect of my life. I lived an *urgent* Christian life. My devotional life was fervent, and I boldly shared Christ with all those around me. Our battle cry in those days was two ancient Aramaic words, "*Marana tha.*" They mean "Come, Lord!" We prayed every day for the return of our King.

Where has all the Hope gone? Where are the zealots? There has never been a time when Hope was more desperately needed than today. We live in a Hope-drained world that is filled with despair. Hope takes the glow of our confidence and puts it on public display. Jesus commanded it. Hope motivates a positive outlook on life. "You are the light of the world. A city set on a hill cannot be hidden; nor does anyone light a lamp and put it under a basket, but on the lampstand, and it gives light to all who are in the house. Let your light shine before men in such a way that they may see your good works, and glorify your Father who is in heaven" (Matthew 5:14-16).

A LESSON IN FALSE HOPE

On May 30, 1987, I was at home, finishing breakfast on a bright, sunny Saturday morning, when I received a most unusual phone call.

The unfamiliar voice began, "Pastor, I know you do not know me, but I am the chief of security for Muhammad Ali, and we are here in Las Vegas for the Mike Tyson–Pinklon Thomas heavyweight title fight."

Okay, I thought, *What has this got to do with me?*

He continued on in an excited voice, "I am a Christian, my bride is arriving in town this afternoon, and we need a pastor to conduct the ceremony."

My first thought was, "Talk about last-minute planning!" I quizzically asked, "Don't you have a pastor?"

"Oh yes," he exclaimed. "We went through premarital counseling and all that, but now something has come up at the last minute and he is not able to come."

His voice carried a tone of desperation as he went on with his story. "Pastor, everyone that is important to me is in town for the wedding and I have to find a pastor to marry us. I know I could find a Justice of the Peace, here in Las Vegas, but we are Christians. We want a Christian ceremony."

He won me over. I responded, "I totally understand and would be happy to conduct the ceremony. Tell me the details."

He told me that the wedding would be held that afternoon at the Las Vegas Hilton in Muhammad Ali's suite. Then he dropped a bombshell. "Muhammad Ali will be my best man."

A lot of interesting things happen to you when you pastor in a city like Las Vegas, but this one was right up there near the top. I immediately thought of my brother, who was an avid boxing fan, and asked, "My brother is a huge fan of Ali's, is it okay if he comes along?"

He assured me that it would be totally fine. On the way to the wedding, I stopped by to get my brother Andy who was anxiously waiting. He was crammed into his only sports jacket, at least a size too small, and had a big smile on his face. We were not sure if the wedding story was totally legit, but we headed off with high hopes for a most excellent adventure.

True to his word, the groom met us in front of the suite and invited us in. He informed us that the bride had been delayed at the airport but she would be there soon. I looked around the room and noticed some faces you see associated with boxing on television. In a few moments Ali emerged from an adjoining room and began entertaining all of us with some amateur magic tricks.

The groom pulled me aside and gave me some passionate instructions for the wedding. "Pastor," he said, "everyone that is important to me is in this room. I want them to have an opportunity to hear about Christ. I will start the wedding by sharing my personal testimony of how Christ has changed my life. Then I want you to share about Jesus Christ and what he can do for them." He encouraged me with the enthusiasm of a new believer. "Please, Pastor, do not hold back."

The smile of a sports fan being invited into the locker room crossed my face. "Don't worry, I will not hold back," I assured him.

The bride arrived and the informal wedding began. The groom nervously faced the audience with tears in his eyes, and in a faltering voice began to tell his story. "You have all known me," he started. "I know that you have seen the change in my life that Jesus has made."

I could not help but glance over to Ali's face to see if there was a reaction. He was unreadable.

The groom shared a few more thoughts and finished his short talk with the words, "I want you to know that Jesus can do the same for you."

Then it was my turn. I remember thinking, "Go for it, dude!" I mean, how many times would I get to share the truth of God with Muhammad Ali and this crowd? I picked up where the groom had left off as a boldness of the Holy Spirit came over me. I finished my short message with a sense that hearts had been touched. I then continued the wedding ceremony and concluded by pronouncing them man and wife. They kissed and we were done.

A few moments later, while I was looking at happy newlyweds, I felt a large hand settle over my shoulder. It was Ali. He was holding a paper he had written about the prophet Muhammad. He signed it in front of me, handed it to me and asked me what I thought about it.

I scanned the front page and immediately saw where it was headed. I looked Ali in the eye and told him, "Ali, this is a lie. You can't follow both Jesus and Muhammad. Jesus said, 'I am the way, the truth, and the life; no man comes to the Father but by me.' You can't accept Jesus as just another prophet. He was either God as he claimed, or he was a madman and a liar."

I had to lean in and listen carefully to understand his diminished speech. We entered into a meaningful exchange about the claims of Christ. We were so engaged that he lost track of time. The groom re-donned his chief of security role and urgently shouted, "Ali, it is time, we have to go down to the fight. We have to leave now!"

Ali asked for my phone number, and then asked if I would come down to watch the fight. I was taken aback and then remembered my brother. "I would love to, Ali," I said and then pointed to Andy. "My brother is here. Can he come too?"

Ali waved him over, and we headed down to the fight, nestled in the midst of Ali's entourage. The Hilton had set up a temporary but huge outdoor arena to host the world championship fight. We entered one end of the arena at a precisely choreographed moment, before the start of the fight. I stood next to Ali as we waited just inside the entrance.

It was not long before those closest to us began to point in our direction. A faint but increasing murmur began to bring the crowd to life as they recognized Ali.

"Ali, Ali!" the crowd began to chant. More and more people turned to see the source of the commotion and joined in the chant. Before long the entire stadium was pulsing "Ali, Ali." It was deafening and somewhat awe-inspiring.

I turned my head and looked into the eyes of Muhammad Ali. I had expected to see the self-satisfied smile of a man glowing in the adoration of the crowd. I do not pretend to know what was going on in his mind, but his face surprised me. His eyes appeared empty. It seemed as if all the praises of men could not fill them up.

A passage of Scripture came to mind. It reminded me of the futility of living a life without Christ. "For when he dies he will carry nothing away; His glory will not descend after him. Though while he lives he congratulates himself—And though men praise you when you do well for yourself" (Psalm 49:17-18).

A VISION OF DESTINY

God gave me a gift that day. I realized that no matter how many accolades one could ever hope to receive in this life, they are incapable of satisfying the soul. I had seen this in the face of one of the most revered athletes in the world. Pride's empty promises were exposed. Its end is despair. Everything is but a fleeting shadow in the face of eternal life.

Hope lifts an otherwise earthbound soul above the empty promises and deceitful lusts of this world. When Hope increases, temporal things start to lose their shine. Hope apprehends a glimpse of glory, from which we can never fully recover. It beholds the King and the glories of his everlasting kingdom.

Life is not about self-aggrandizement or personal achievements that feed the ego. Life is about glorifying God with all our faculties. Abilities and resources are offerings that we give back to God. Worship goes far beyond enthusiastic singing. It is a life of service and obedience. Paul urged this Hope-filled approach to life: "I urge you, brethren, by the mercies of God, to present your bodies a living and holy sacrifice, acceptable to God, which is your spiritual service of worship" (Romans 12:1).

Hope instills a vision of destiny. It makes us pilgrims and strangers on this earth. Our dreams become focused on a new world and a coming King. The Bible highlights this spiritual character condition: "For you showed sympathy to the prisoners and accepted joyfully the seizure of your property, knowing that you have for yourselves a better possession and a lasting one" (Hebrews 10:34).

Hope is addicted to the future. It sees a sunrise beyond the sunset of this life. Hope is not wishful thinking, but optimism rooted in an optimal reality. As the author of Hebrews instructs, "We receive a kingdom which cannot be shaken" (Hebrews 12:28).

World economies will struggle. Our health must eventually decline. Troubles will surely come. Hope empowers the soul to rise above the storm clouds that would diminish bright heavenly skies. Hope is an essential part of our spirituality. Without it we would be irreparably crippled and suffer a malformed character.

THE SYMPTOMATIC VIRTUES

Hope has specific attitudes and behaviors that are associated with it. When you put the character traits together, they paint an incredible mosaic of Hope. The Bible provides an inventory of Hope symptoms. Figure 9.1 illustrates many of the symptomatic character traits that radiate out of a Hope-filled heart. As we have seen, it is essential to understand the relationship between our symptoms and the root causes behind what we do. Once we understand the difference between causes and symptoms, it delivers us from the fruitless pursuit of chasing symptoms. We are freed to focus our energies on the motivations that can change our lives.

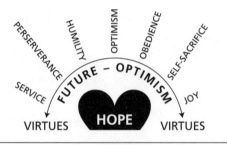

Figure 9.1

Are you struggling with a lack of joy? The prescription "Cheer up!" doesn't work. Do you feel like giving up? Platitudes lack the motivational power to help you. How do you increase in joy? A joy problem is a Hope problem. Hope cannot help but put a smile on the face of those who possess it. If you want more staying power, increase your Hope quotient.

Do you lack the ability to say no to yourself? You already know the slogan "Just say no" doesn't work. What is needed is a good dose of Hope. Dramatic things happen when our souls are captivated by "things which eye has not seen and ear has not heard, and which have not entered the heart of man, all that God has prepared for those who love him" (1 Corinthians 2:9).

Hope apprehends a sure and certain future. Hope is a strong reality anchor that holds firm against the deceptive currents and popular tides of this world. "This hope we have as an anchor of the soul, a hope both sure and steadfast" (Hebrews 6:19).

THE HOPE CONTINUUM

Figure 9.2 illustrates the balance of Hope. It is a more detailed view of the power zone graphic in chapter four. There are two slippery slopes on either side of true Hope: the diminishment of Hope and the hyping up of Hope.

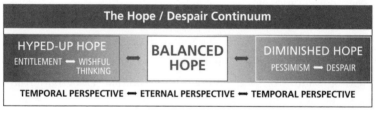

Figure 9.2

Everyone understands how Hope becomes diminished. The loss of a job, a bad diagnosis, news of an accident—earthly hopes can be suddenly crushed. True Hope, which is rooted in eternal truths, is uncrushable.

Hyped-up Hope is less understood. It is a form of religious extremism that heads in one of two directions. In one case, it can lead to an inappropriate disengagement from the world. Practitioners become so heavenly minded that they are no earthly good. True Hope remains firmly engaged with the realities of the world. In another case, hyped hope can become enamored of the attractions of this world. Believers engage in wishful thinking and become filled with a sense of earthly entitlements that undermine the spirit of true Hope. There is more enthusiasm to claim earthly dreams than to celebrate heavenly realities. Balanced Hope resides in the middle of the power zone, where it continues to abound by the power of the

Holy Spirit. In the next chapter we will explore in much greater detail the balance and the imbalances of Hope.

AN ETERNAL PERSPECTIVE

Why is true Hope always very engaged in this world? Future realities demand it. Jesus described the intrusion of Hope into our mundane daily lives. "Whoever in the name of a disciple gives to one of these little ones even a cup of cold water to drink, truly I say to you, he shall not lose his reward" (Matthew 10:42). If a simple act of kindness like that guarantees a reward, imagine what a life dedicated to serving others could produce!

Every true believer has tasted of the powers of the world to come. If you are a Christian, Hope has touched your life. Making spiritual progress means that we continue on the path where our values increasingly shift from the temporal to the eternal. Hope powerfully motivates us to continue the journey.

Those whom Hope has captivated become more and more positive as they age. I have had the privilege to hold the hands of spiritually mature believers at the end of their journey. They possess a joyful expectation to see the things that the Spirit has convinced them of throughout their lives.

I have also been with those who have placed all their priorities and hopes in this world. It is often a bitter end. Their pessimism gives way to despair. The end of life teaches a person a lot about life. More people should stand at deathbeds, observe and reflect on their own lives.

The Bible instructs us to judge ourselves. No one has perfect Hope. No believer is devoid of Hope. Where do you think you would score on the Hope continuum? Where have you placed your hopes? Do you seek the praises of people or of God? What are the rewards you hold most dear?

THE FIELD OF CONTENTION FOR HOPE

Figure 9.3 shows the full spectrum of character traits that are associated with Hope or the lack of it. The Motivational Virtue of Hope is positioned against the Motivational Evil of the pride of life in the image of a divided heart.

Figure 9.3

In many ways the motivational forces of Hope and Pride are opposites of one another. Hope is captivated by a compelling glorious future. The pride of life is all about establishing my glory in the present.

These opposing motivations, as you can see, produce very different personality traits and behaviors in people. One leads to optimism and the other to pessimism. One is a joyful servant while the other is a prideful ruler. One is a positive encourager while the other is arrogant and critical of others. You might ask yourself, "Which kind of person would I prefer to hang out with?" Pride of life personality types are attracted to people who must feed their ego. They lack consideration and rarely think about the needs of others. Hope-filled people stick with you for the long haul. They are steady, encouraging friends.

Hope and the pride of life are locked in a deadly war, battling for dominion over your heart. The pride of life pulls you in the direction of your present accomplishments and worldly dreams; Hope pulls you in the direction of your eternal future. The one you feed the most is the one that wins the most.

Figure 9.3 is a simple visual model that depicts the struggle of Hope. See the areas of Hope that represent present areas of growth. Do you struggle with pride? Are you critical or an encourager of others? The answers to these questions provide a basis for a quick snapshot of your Hope quotient. Assessing yourself—or as the Bible states, "judging yourself"—is the key to staying on track in the pursuit of your personal growth objectives.

SELF-DENIAL

We would miss it if we failed to address one of the great hallmarks of Hope. Hope empowers the practice of sustained self-denial. This character trait is one of the deepest evidences of a Hope-filled heart. The apostle Paul personified this capacity to the extreme. What was the secret to his unflagging motivation?

Paul clarifies the things that were *not* a motivation to him: "If from human motives I fought with wild beasts at Ephesus, what does it profit me? If the dead are not raised, let us eat and drink, for to-morrow we die" (1 Corinthians 15:32). Human motives are not Paul's motives. There is no human explanation for his ability to endure hardship. Paul further clarifies his motives a few verses above in the same passage: "If we have hoped in Christ in this life only, we are of all men most to be pitied" (1 Corinthians 15:19).

The key phrase here is "in this life only." Why does Paul take the hard way when so many others head down the easy path? He looked to the end game. His Hope was grounded in another world. He apprehended the future and it apprehended him.

Self-denial, for a man like Paul, was as natural as self-advancement is for a pride-filled man. Paul denied himself and endured much through the motivational power of Hope. "We are afflicted in every way, but not crushed; perplexed, but not despairing" (2 Corinthians 4:8).

FINAL THOUGHTS

Hope is perhaps the least understood of the Motivational Virtues. In most churches much more attention is directed toward Love and Faith. This is something that must be corrected. Hope is one of the three primary, positive motivational forces in the world. It contributes to and energizes a vital aspect of healthy character development.

The underemphasis of Hope in the church today is particularly disturbing given the times in which we live. It is a period of history in which people are fiscally distraught through poverty and fiscally distracted through the promise of prosperity. Predictably, despair has become an epidemic. The expansion of the global economy into China and Third World countries has spread the message of entitlement faster than the gospel of Jesus Christ. The Bible predicted a day when humankind would be in its present condition.

> But realize this, that in the last days difficult times will come. For men will be lovers of self, lovers of money, boastful, arrogant, revilers, disobedient to parents, ungrateful, unholy, unloving, irreconcilable, malicious gossips, without self-control, brutal, haters of good, treacherous, reckless, conceited, lovers of pleasure rather than lovers of God. (2 Timothy 3:1-4)

Many Hope-reduced Christians look at the zealous Hope of young believers and tolerantly smile. "Just wait until they have been around for a while. They will calm down and gain a more seasoned perspective." If by "seasoned" you mean that my Hope of a glorious eternal future filled with divine rewards will cease energizing my daily life, "No thank you, sir!" I would rather remain as a child, waiting for the sound of my Father's return.

Embrace the Motivational Virtue of Hope. Walk in the contexts of the Spirit, the Word and community where God can speak to you about Hope. Find the right mixes of spiritual disciplines that work for you. Let the Spirit cause you to abound in Hope. It will define your character and change everything about your life.

Hope offends the sensibilities of those who have been lulled by the comforts and selfish pursuits of this world. This should not surprise us. Hope is high-octane fuel. It is powerful stuff and not for those who want to remain unradicalized by the gospel of Jesus Christ.

10

THE DISTORTIONS OF HOPE

Hope Imbalances and the Power Zone

> *You may say I'm a dreamer,*
> *but I'm not the only one.*
> *I hope someday you'll join us.*
> *And the world will live as one.*
>
> John Lennon

> *Fix your hope completely on the grace to be*
> *brought to you at the revelation of Jesus Christ.*
>
> 1 Peter 1:13

Hope is the most resilient stuff in the universe. Attack it and it bounces back. Try to crush it and it smiles. Put it under pressure and it keeps on keeping on.

The apostle Paul was a buffed-up man of Hope. Beat him with rods, bind him in chains, place him in jail, and watch him sing (Acts 16:22-30). Stone him, drag him out of the city, leave him for dead and watch him walk back into the city (Acts 14:19-20). The greater the adversity, the more it encouraged him to rejoice in the future. Observe his calm demeanor on the heaving deck of a storm-tossed ship. Listen with rapt attention, along with 276 fear-filled shipmates, to Paul's confident message of Hope: "Therefore I encourage you to take some food, for this is for your preservation, for not a hair from the head of any of you will perish" (Acts 27:34). Nothing got him off balance. When blessed, he humbled himself. When humbled, he blessed God.

While imprisoned, Paul wrote a short letter to the church at Philippi. It was primarily a message of Hope. Three keynote phrases set the tone.

1. "He who began a good work in you will perfect it until the day of Christ Jesus" (Philippians 1:6).

2. "Be sincere and blameless until the day of Christ" (Philippians 1:10).

3. "Holding fast the word of life, so that in the day of Christ I will have reason to glory" (Philippians 2:16).

Why this fixation on "the day of Christ"? It is Hope thinking. It was Paul's perspective on life. *Today* is all about living for the *great and coming day*. Hope puts every day within that context. Paul was motivated by the future and rooted in the present.

Christ-Hope is long-sighted. It sees beyond the temporal bumps in the road and embraces the eternal. It is not just countercultural. It is out of this world.

THE NECESSITY OF HOPE

Human nature needs hope. People cling to their hopes, even false ones. They have to. Hopelessness is not a viable option. Hope is the foundation upon which every human enterprise has been built. Without Hope, no businesses would be started, no investments would be made, no relationships would be entered into and no children would be planned. Hope gets people out of bed in the morning and motivates them to go to work.

There is nothing more demoralizing than losing one's Hope. It utterly paralyzes the human spirit. This reality looms large given the Hope crisis in our troubled world.

Cursed Hope. The question now is, "In what do you hope?" If you have placed all your hopes in this world, you are bound for certain despair. "The world is passing away, and also its lusts; but the one who does the will of God lives forever" (1 John 2:17).

Jesus overturns the tables of earthly lusts. He angered the moneychangers who peddled their goods in ancient Israel's temple (John 2:14-16). In the same way, moneychangers from every nation will be embittered by his return. They will experience the loss of all worldly hope. The Day of the Lord is coming: "Behold, He is coming with the clouds, and every eye will see Him, even those who pierced Him; and all the tribes of the earth will mourn over Him. So it is to be" (Revelation 1:7).

Earthly Hopes will be dashed. Billions will mourn. The wealth of this world will evaporate.

Blessed Hope. Others will have a totally opposite experience at the return of Christ. Shouts of praise will erupt around the globe. Hope will be realized beyond their wildest imaginations.

> For the Lord Himself will descend from heaven with a shout, with the voice of the archangel and with the trumpet of God, and the dead in Christ will rise first. Then we who are alive and remain will be caught up together with them in the clouds to meet the Lord in the air, and so we shall always be with the Lord. Therefore comfort one another with these words. (1 Thessalonians 4:16-18)

Hope is a source of unending comfort. When you get down, look up! The day of Christ is coming!

THE WONDER OF HOPE

Imagine what it would be like for an ancient Roman leader to stand in Times Square, in the shadows of high-rises with cars rushing by and jets flying overhead. The things that man has prepared over the last two thousand years of technological advancements would be beyond belief to him. Return him to his world, and he would lack the words to adequately describe it.

This is nothing compared to the amazing surprises that are in store for God's kids. God has been preparing a place for us for two thousand years. He is not limited by the constraints of time like we are. Jesus promised, "I go and prepare a place for you, I will come again and receive you to Myself, that where I am, there you may be also" (John 14:3). The accomplishments of man, impressive as they may be, are nothing compared to the creative genius of God, who made the universe. Try to imagine what that means! Paul exults over the possibilities: "Things which eye has not seen and ear has not heard, and which have not entered the heart of man, all that *God has prepared* for those who love him" (1 Corinthians 2:9).

If someone visited heaven and stood in the middle of it, they would be unable to describe its wonders to us back on earth. I sense this when I read John's attempts to describe heavenly realities. The images in the book of Revelation are largely incomprehensible. John may have been unable to adequately describe heaven, but his wonder and excitement come through loud and clear. You can almost see him trembling as he writes:

> Immediately I was in the Spirit; and behold, a throne was standing in heaven, and One sitting on the throne. And He who was sitting was like a jasper stone and a sardius in appearance; and there was a rainbow around the throne, like an emerald in appearance. Around the throne were twenty-four thrones; and upon the thrones I saw twenty-four elders sitting, clothed in

white garments, and golden crowns on their heads. (Revelation 4:2-4)

Hope is not just positive thinking. Hope embraces a world of coming wonders. Get excited!

FALSE HOPES

Our modern age is very much like all of history. Even with our technological prowess and educational advancements, the human spirit remains the same insecure, lustful creature that it was thousands of years ago. The three great isms—materialism, hedonism and egotism (see chapter three)—have ruled the human heart since the rebellion of Adam and Eve.

John describes the human condition this way: "For all that is in the world, the lust of the flesh [hedonism] and the lust of the eyes [materialism] and the boastful pride of life [egotism], is not from the Father, but is from the world" (1 John 2:16). This is the "why" behind what we do.

In the previous verse, John tells us what we should do: "Do not love the world nor the things in the world" (1 John 2:15). This creates a huge dilemma for multitudes of people. How can I not place my affections on the world? What is left? The world to come!

Hopeless materialism. Place your hope in personal wealth if you must. Know that it will surely fail you. It may not occur during your earning years, but it will surely happen at the end of life. Disbursal day comes. There you, like everyone who has gone before, must leave everything behind. Jesus spoke of one such rich man: "You fool! This very night your soul is required of you; and now who will own what you have prepared?" (Luke 12:20).

The stock market crash and the global financial crisis, which began to manifest in the fall of 2008, ushered in a wave of anxiety and despair. Hopelessness has the power to paralyze a human heart or a world economy. Financial stress is difficult for everyone. Christ-Hope means we are never bankrupt. Account balances continue to grow. Better days are ahead.

There is no devaluation of currency, inflation, loss of investment, poor fiscal management, managerial greed, Wall Street cronyism, financial panic or fear in heaven. Jesus outlined Hope's investment plan: "Store up for yourselves treasures in heaven, where neither moth nor rust destroys, and where thieves do not break in or steal" (Matthew 6:20).

Wealth can be a stumbling block. The need for Hope applies equally to the rich and poor. "Instruct those who are rich in this present world not to be conceited or to fix their hope on the uncertainty of riches, but on God, who richly supplies us with all things to enjoy" (1 Timothy 6:17).

Hopeless hedonism. Hedonism has no time for the delayed gratification of Hope. It wants to be happy—*now*. It lives in the moment. Like a butterfly, it flits from one experience to the next in an unending search for pleasure. Instantaneous gratification is the order of the day. Hedonism holds vast multitudes of the young firmly in its grip. They party with no thoughts for tomorrow. Hedonism's only desire is to experience more short-term fun, pleasure and excitement.

Time is not on hedonism's side. One day, far sooner then its followers realize, the hopes of hedonism will begin to fail. Their body will age. Fleshly lusts will no longer satisfy. God gave humankind a short lifespan for a reason. Our mortality gives Hope many opportunities to blossom in the midst of our foolish pursuits. "Live the rest of the time in the flesh no longer for the lusts of men, but for the will of God. For the time already past is sufficient for you to have carried out the desire of the Gentiles, having pursued a course of sensuality, lusts, drunkenness, carousing, drinking parties and abominable idolatries" (1 Peter 4:2-3).

Hope matures our character. It makes us farsighted. We start to live like the eternal beings we are.

Hopeless egotism. Pride is the most ignorant of vices. It is prime evidence that people have lost their way in the universe. The arrogant live like people in the Dark Ages who believed that the sun revolved around the earth. Pride acts out a belief system that says, "I am the center of the universe and everything should revolve around me."

Pride finds root in many things: achievements, position, education, power, talent, appearance, intellect, wealth or ability. Pride is self-promoting. It compares itself with others. It devalues other people. In so doing it ultimately devalues its bearer. Pride is a misdirected search for significance. It is a driving lust for importance. Its quest for greatness is its undoing.

Pride's desires are misdirected. There is nothing you can do to increase your inherent value and worth as a person. God has already made you a being of great destiny. Stop striving. King David marveled:

> When I consider Your heavens, the work of Your fingers,
> The moon and the stars, which You have ordained;
> What is man that You take thought of him,
> And the son of man that You care for him?
> Yet You have made him a little lower than God,
> And You crown him with glory and majesty!
> You make him to rule over the works of Your hands;
> You have put all things under his feet. (Psalm 8:3-6)

Christ is coming to set an upside-down world right-side up. The servant will be the master. The humble will be exalted. God will be praised. The prideful will be humbled. "At the name of Jesus every knee will bow, of those who are in heaven and on earth and under the earth, and that every tongue will confess that Jesus Christ is Lord, to the glory of God the Father" (Philippians 2:10-11).

Hope has grasped a grand view of a God-centered universe. It empowers people to celebrate their self-worth. Humble yourself and God will exalt you in "the day of Christ."

THE POSITIVE PERSONA

The balanced Hope graphic in figure 10.1 is the same model used to illustrate balanced Faith in the previous chapter and will be used in the upcoming chapter on Love. The positive persona graphic illustrates the balances of Hope between obedience and service. Professed obedience to Christ without service toward others is self-deception. It is inhumane Hope. How can someone claim to be a Christ follower and not follow in his footsteps? Obedience and service represent the harmonious balance of genuine Hope. As we have seen, there is an unbreakable correlation between how we relate to God and how we relate to people.

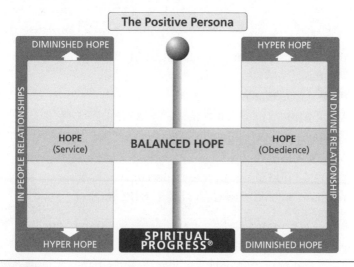

Figure 10.1

Relating to God. Hope takes the promises of God to the bank. Hope knows that all blessings and every adversity is just a passing condition that is unrelated to the real welfare of our souls. Prosperity's and poverty's greatest value is that they serve to test the purity of our Hope. Both conditions reveal a lot about what motivates us. The apostle Paul was a great model of a Hope-motivated life. His words are as relevant today as they were when he wrote them. "I know how to get along with humble means, and I also know how to live in prosperity; in any and every circumstance I have learned the secret of being filled and going hungry, both of having abundance and suffering need" (Philippians 4:12).

What was Paul's secret? He was neither impressed with money nor discouraged by its absence. He was so taken with eternal Hope that he put no great stock in the things of this world. Only Hope-filled people can utter the following words of Paul: "I have learned to be content in whatever circumstances I am" (Philippians 4:11).

Do you want to be truly rich? Eternal perspectives make people think and act very differently about life. Listen to Hope's attitude, once again, through the timeless words of Paul: "But godliness actually is a means of great gain when accompanied by contentment. For we have brought nothing into the world, so we cannot take anything out of it either. If we have food and covering, with these we shall be content" (1 Timothy 6:6-8).

Hope has fastened its tenacious grip on the generosity of God. It raises the banners of joy and endurance in its service to God. Hope understands that this life is a short opportunity to utilize God's gifts. It is determined to produce a many-fold return on the Creator's investments in us.

Relating to people. Jesus said of himself, "The Son of Man did not come to be served, but to serve" (Matthew 20:28). Hope has a transforming effect on the way we view people. The day of Christ is coming. The more we believe it and start to prepare for it, the more our fixation on temporal things is broken. Selfish living loses its luster and we are motivated to bless others.

Hope sees the world as it will be and acts accordingly. There are no rich or poor, there are no great and mighty, for "every knee will bow" (Philippians 2:10). My personal rights take second place to God's purposes. God's will becomes paramount. Hope lives in a world where every cup of water given in Jesus' name will receive a sure reward. It instructs that every kindness, every act of generosity, and every consideration for "the least of these" is building a better tomorrow.

THE DISTRACTED PERSONA

The distracted persona is the picture of what happens when one's Hope begins to become diminished. Diminished Hope impacts the way we relate to God and to people.

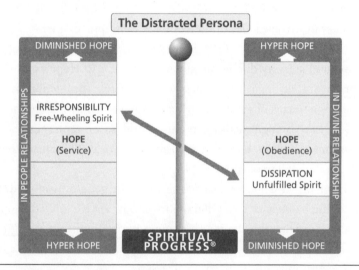

Figure 10.2

Relating to God. There are countless distractions that compete for the interest of our souls. When Hope begins to wane it has a predictable impact on one's perspective and relationship with God. Diminished Hope, like diminished Faith and Love, distances us from the purposes of God.

The human spirit is so constructed that it must be fed by Hope. If

Christ-Hope wanes, then other hopes will move in to fill the vacuum. Even a small shift in the focus of one's hopes can have big ramifications on the way we live our lives. Jesus spoke of the either-or battle of Hope in one of his famous sermons: "No one can serve two masters; for either he will hate the one and love the other, or he will be devoted to one and despise the other. You cannot serve God and wealth" (Matthew 6:24). Christ-Hope-filled people are naturally devoted to God. Christ-Hope-diminished people suffer from an intolerable void of purpose. They search to fill it with some form or meaning.

Relating to people. Diminished Hope erodes a person's desire to serve others. Tasks that seemed joyful become wearisome. Selfish motivations compete for our loyalties. Personal pursuits replace enthusiastic volunteerism.

Low Hope has a big impact on a church. It impacts congregational morale and causes the dysfunctional church syndrome where 20 percent of the people do 80 percent of the work. No one wants to volunteer. Life is too exciting to waste time at church. Show me a church that has an ongoing volunteer crisis and I will show you a church that scores low on a corporate Hope assessment.

Low Hope means that the promise of eternal rewards has lost out to instant gratifications. What about that reward that Jesus promised for even small acts of service like giving a cup of cold water? It's free. Anyone can afford to participate. It carries with it the weight of a heavenly reward. Sorry! Hearts are enthralled elsewhere.

Besides individual assessments, SpiritualProgress.com offers church-wide, cumulative character assessments.

The first outward evidence of diminished Hope in God is a withdrawal from *serving* others. Kingdom sensibilities have been replaced by the love of the world. The diminishment of the Motivational Virtue of Hope opens the door to evil. The hopes of this world rush in to fill the void. Motivations shift. An important part of a person's character is defined by the source of their hope.

Hope is our anchor. It keeps us moored to eternal realities. We see the world as it is. "For it is for this we labor and strive, because we have fixed our hope on the living God, who is the Savior of all men" (1 Timothy 4:10).

THE FRENZIED PERSONA

The frenzied persona illustrates what happens when Hope becomes severely diminished. As the word *frenzied* implies, is a very unsatisfied place for the heart. The Bible instructs, "This hope we have as an anchor of the soul, a hope both sure and steadfast" (Hebrews 6:19). Diminished Hope has lost its moorings with God and is adrift in a sea of empty promises. At this stage it is not uncommon for previously religious people to begin ravenous pursuits of worldly hopes. The heart is constructed in such a way that it clamors for hope, any hope. It will not be denied. This is one of the great human vulnerabilities to evil.

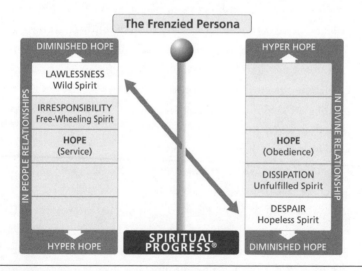

Figure 10.3

Relating to God. The impact of severely diminished Hope is predictably damaging to one's relationship with God. What began as dissipation and distraction has led to discouragement and despair. The frenzied persona finds itself flailing about in a desperate search for significance. God seems a million miles away.

The way back to Hope, at this stage, often takes a life-changing crisis. Others awaken from spiritual darkness at the end of life. It is never too late! In one's darkest moment, when all worldly hopes have failed, God is waiting. He never left! He uses our eventual death as a course instructor for life. Why wait? Put your Hope in Christ now!

Relating to people. People with an advanced condition of diminished Hope relate to others in a very distinct way. Any pretense to serve others has long been replaced with a deep-rooted commitment to serve one's self-interests. The soul is too unsatisfied to give much thought to satisfying the needs of others. This path leads to one place—further Hopelessness. Self is a puny god with a Hopeless future.

There is a path back to Hope-filled relationships. It is a radical cure. The treatment is so severe that few take it. But it's simple— become a slave. Take your eyes off your own unfulfilled needs and serve others. Serving can open one's eyes to unexpected joys. Volunteer to feed the poor. You will find God standing in line, in the midst of serving others. Jesus taught us how to find him.

> Then the King will say . . . "Come, you who are blessed of My Father, inherit the kingdom prepared for you from the foundation of the world. For I was hungry, and you gave Me something to eat; I was thirsty, and you gave Me something to drink; I was a stranger, and you invited Me in; naked, and you clothed Me; I was sick, and you visited Me; I was in prison, and you came to Me." Then the righteous will answer Him, "Lord, when did we see You hungry, and feed You, or thirsty, and give You something to drink? And when did we see You a stranger,

and invite You in, or naked, and clothe You? When did we see You sick, or in prison, and come to You?" The King will answer and say to them, "Truly I say to you, to the extent that you did it to one of these brothers of Mine, even the least of them, you did it to Me." (Matthew 25:34-40)

Serving people is serving God. Hope is the kind of supercharged motivational condition that can transform a selfish person into a true slave of Christ. In the world to come, things will look very different. Slaves will be kings. The least will be the greatest. Start serving today!

THE INFLATED PERSONA

The inflated persona is the picture of what happens when one's Hope begins to become hyped up. Hyper Hope impacts the way we relate to God and to people. Hyper Hope has headed in the opposite direction of hopelessness. It looks like Hope but is as self-serving as diminished Hope. How does it come into existence?

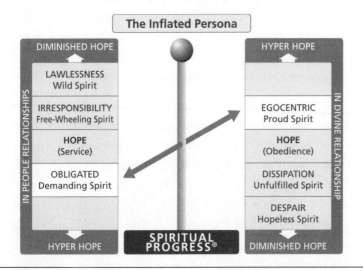

Figure 10.4

If the devil, the "angel of light," cannot distract someone from passionate Hope in the coming kingdom of God, then he has one more option. He can spin the virtue of Hope into a confused distortion of the real thing. Hyper Hope looks like the real thing, only more of it. Isn't more better? Those who have entered the devil's spin zone know how convincing this lie can be.

The inflated persona has bought into some paper-thin theology. Like Adam and Eve in the Garden, they have a partial grasp of the truth. We know from history just how dangerous this can be. Pride is the doorway into hyper Hope. Experience a little spiritual growth. Gain a few victories. Shazam! You start to feel like a genuine spiritual giant! Misinterpret a few Bible verses, listen to your ego, and the transformation is well underway.

Healthy character development maintains a balance between diminished Hope and hyper Hope. How can you discern the difference? The answer is simple. Examine the caliber of a person's relationships. Let's look first at the God side.

Relating to God. Hyper Hope misses the main point. Christ-Hope sees the world like John the Baptist. He, like us, was called to usher in the kingdom of Christ. Observe his heart toward Christ: "He must increase, but I must decrease" (John 3:30).

Christ-Hope is consumed with the majesty of Christ and the glory of his coming kingdom. The privilege of my participation humbles me. I gain confidence from being a part of something that is far greater than myself.

Hyper Hope twists everything around. It says, "I must increase so Christ can increase." It lacks appropriate humility. It confuses humble obedience with an elevated sense of self-importance. Hyper Hope starts down a path of "I am awesome" devotion. Particular attention is given to showcasing the depth of one's spirituality to others.

Relating to others. In hyper Hope, the motivation for serving others emanates from an egocentric source. It congratulates itself on all that it does for God. It cries, "Look at me!" Authentic Hope, in contrast, is amazed at God's grace. It knows it is utterly unworthy, yet it has been granted the astounding privilege of being a servant of God. It has three distinctive traits that validate its authenticity.

1. Service is worship. It is a joy-filled enterprise.

2. Service is personally fulfilling. Service is its own reward.

3. Service lays no obligations on those it serves. It is selfless.

Egocentric service can be identified by three different traits.

1. It fulfills one's duty. Service becomes obligatory.

2. It needs the accolades of others. Service needs praise.

3. It expects others to serve at their level of commitment. Service grants the power to manipulate and judge others.

Hyper Hope is a soul condition that is in the process of losing its way. It meanders on a sea of false expectations toward God and others.

THE SUPERIOR PERSONA

The superior persona is a picture of what happens when one's Hope becomes severely hyped up. Extreme hyper Hope has a huge impact on the way we relate to God and others. The superior persona represents someone who has slipped into the most extreme form of self-serving religion. At this stage of imbalance, the heart and mind have become locked in a highly defended belief system that is very difficult to penetrate. Not only are they proud about the way they serve God, but their way is also the *only* way to serve God. They are shrewd at making rules that empower them to manipulate and control others.

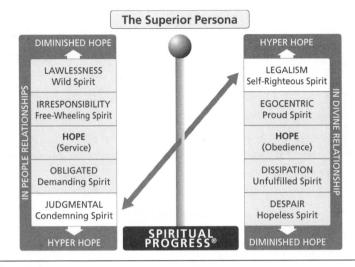

Figure 10.5

The Pharisees were a group of religious people in the Bible who embodied a superior persona. They focused on the visible and noteworthy opportunities for service. This coincidentally allowed others to see and applaud their extreme devotion.

Self-aggrandizement is a hallmark of egocentric service. The Pharisees personified it. Jesus confronted it. "But they do all their deeds to be noticed by men; for they broaden their phylacteries and lengthen the tassels of their garments. They love the place of honor at banquets and the chief seats in the synagogues, and respectful greetings in the market places, and being called Rabbi by men" (Matthew 23:5-7).

It is worthwhile to note that there is not one occasion in the Bible where the Pharisees were presented in a positive light. There is *nothing* positive to say about this spiritual condition.

THE WAY HOME

There is a path back to building authentic Hope. It is a radical cure for those who have become addicted to the praises of others. It is a severe treatment regimen for a severe problem. Jesus prescribed it: Do your serving where no one can see it. This is a part of the spiritual discipline of secrecy explained in chapter six.

Invisible service is largely thankless, but it is just what the Great Physician ordered for the soul. You are well on your way when sustained behind-the-scenes service really works for you. It is purifying and liberating. It is building treasure in heaven where God who sees in secret *today* will *tomorrow* reward you openly.

This is a big deal to God. Hope is an essential Motivational Virtue that shapes your character. Pervert it and it has huge ramifications for your life.

No less than five times in one of his sermons, Jesus condemned practicing good deeds to be "noticed by men" (Matthew 6:1, 2, 5, 16, 18). He warned that this kind of service has no Hope of future rewards associated with it. "Beware of practicing your righteousness before men to be noticed by them; otherwise you have no reward with your Father who is in heaven" (Matthew 6:1).

Jesus' sermon advocates the practice of invisible service in a way no one could misunderstand its meaning. I would entitle the following thoughts, "The Secret Service of the Christ Follower."

So when you give to the poor, do not sound a trumpet before you, as the hypocrites do in the synagogues and in the streets, so that they may be honored by men. Truly I say to you, they have their reward in full. But when you give to the poor, do not let your left hand know what your right hand is doing, so that your giving will be in secret; and your Father who sees what is done in secret will reward you. When you pray, you are not to be like the hypocrites; for they love to stand and pray in the synagogues and on the street corners so that they may be seen by men. Truly I say to you, they have their reward in full. But you, when you pray, go into your inner room, close your door and pray to your Father who is in secret, and your Father who sees what is done in secret will reward you. (Matthew 6:2-6)

Secret service validates the authenticity of balanced Hope.

FINAL THOUGHTS

Much appropriate attention has been given to the meteoric rise of a man with humble single-parent beginnings to the office of the presidency of the United States. Regardless of how you feel about his political values, Barack Obama has walked a journey of Hope. His book, *The Audacity of Hope*, tells some of his remarkable story. But if you really want to talk about the audacity of Hope, I have got a far grander story for you. The rise to the presidency of the United States is nothing compared to this!

An unwanted son was born to a teenage girl and abandoned into the unloving care of an aunt and uncle. The young mother had hidden the existence of her child as if he were some cosmic mistake. She had married into a wealthy family, and his existence would jeopardize her privileged future. The child would never know the identity of the man who had fathered him. Everything about him was a dirty secret. He could read between the lines. He should never have been born.

On the rare occasions that Mom slipped away to visit her abandoned son, he would run into the woods and climb a tall tree. He swayed in the branches, but the cool breeze did nothing to quench the burning of his heart. She was anguished by this, but alas—she loved her way of life more than her son.

The son became a man, fell in love and got married. They had two daughters and a son. It had every appearance of a happy home. The children adored their father. One day, at the age of ten, the son enthusiastically waved to his dad as he drove away from their home. It was beyond his comprehension that he would never see his father again.

The father had found another woman and had decided to move away and live with her. The sins of the unfaithful mother that wounded her son had now devastated her grandchildren. The pain of abandonment had stricken three generations.

The fatherless family was plunged into poverty. They moved into a small apartment. Mom was forced to find the only job available, as a maid in a local hotel. The oldest daughter bore three children out of wedlock. There was not enough room for the son. At the age of fourteen he was forced to live in a boarding house.

I know this story well. The father and the son are my grandfather and my father. My dad still tells stories of the poverty of his childhood.

My mother's father, coincidentally, also abandoned her. He walked into the hospital, had a brief look at the newborn, walked out and was never seen again. My mom's grandparents raised her. Her mother was too involved in complicated relationships to be involved in her life. This was my family legacy.

Predictably, I ended up the product of a broken home. Thankfully my dad overcame his family curse; though my parents divorced, he maintained a strong presence in the lives of his children. Nevertheless, my mother struggled with raising four children as a single parent. I became a lost and wild teenager.

Then one day I met my loving heavenly Father. He is the one who promised, "I will never desert you, nor will I ever forsake you" (Hebrews 13:5). He became my steadfast companion. Everything changed. I saw a purpose for my life. Christ-Hope changed my present and my future.

The product of a broken family was bound for heaven. Wandering was replaced with purpose, loneliness with love, and rebellion with worship. Think of it. A lost kid headed for glory! Adopted into royalty! I am headed for a future where I will rule and reign with Christ forever. Wow! What a reason to get out of bed in the morning.

My story is far from unique. It is the story of every Christ child. It is our family legacy. It is the true audacity of Hope. It is eternal.

11

LOVE
The Giving Virtue

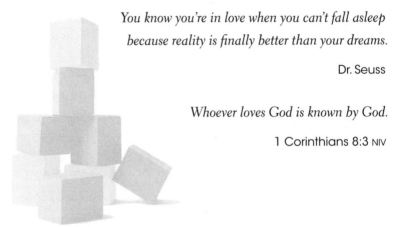

*You know you're in love when you can't fall asleep
because reality is finally better than your dreams.*

Dr. Seuss

Whoever loves God is known by God.

1 Corinthians 8:3 NIV

Love is the virtue that keeps on giving. Nothing can stop the force of its generosity. Nothing!

Jesus personified it. His unwavering generosity in the face of hatred and torture speaks more than eloquent words. His willful surrender demonstrated that nothing could diminish the motivational power of Love.

Peter took a sword and tried to spare Love (John 18:3-12). But Love never needs sparing. Love spares us.

Do you imagine Christ a hapless, helpless victim? Hear his words: "Do you think that I cannot appeal to My Father, and He will at once put at My disposal more than twelve legions of angels?"

(Matthew 26:53). Do the math. A legion is 5,000 Roman soldiers. Imagine the impact of 60,000 (5,000 x 12) angels suddenly arriving on the scene!

Look at the effect that just one angel had on the Roman soldiers guarding Jesus' tomb. "And his appearance was like lightning, and his clothing as white as snow. The guards shook for fear of him and became like dead men" (Matthew 28:3-4). History teaches us that there were likely sixteen guards on duty (Acts 12:4).[1] Again, do the math (60,000 x 16 = 960,000). I see almost a million Roman soldiers (far more than the size of the entire Roman army) lying on the ground like dead men. Jesus had more than enough firepower.

Christ was not captured by hate. He captured a hateful world with Love. Love won.

GOD'S LOVE

Love is a word that means different things to different people. The Greek word used for God's Love, *agape*, has a very unique and specific meaning that is radically different from any earthly concept of Love. Jesus redefined it.[2]

Agape love is so foreign to human experience that it is easiest to describe it by what it is not. It is not the passionate love that a man feels for a woman or a woman for a man. *Eros* is the Greek word for this kind of love, which is common to human experience. Neither does agape love describe the wonderfully altruistic love of a lifelong friend (*phileo*).

Agape Love is an integral part of God's character. It's far more than possessing deep feelings of affection or performing sacrificial deeds. A human heart filled with agape Love visibly represents God's character. This all-encompassing condition captivates and motivates the entire soul.[3] It is a fountainhead from which flow all kinds of positive attitudes and actions.

- Agape starts with healthy self-love: Love forgives one's own personal failures. It restores self-esteem. It celebrates the wonder and sacredness of *every* life, including yours. It offers dignity to all people. "For the whole Law is fulfilled in one word, in the statement, 'You shall love your neighbor as yourself'" (Galatians 5:14).

- Agape is heavenly: Its source is God. It is otherworldly. Don't depend on earthly affirmation. Don't count on others to support you. It's likely you won't be understood. Quiet your soul and hear the heavenly whisper, "This is My beloved Son, in whom I am well-pleased" (Matthew 3:17). "Love is from God" (1 John 4:7).

- Agape is counterintuitive: This Love has some serious explaining to do. It's an upside-down reality. The king is the servant; hatred begets Love. Jesus lived it. "But God demonstrates His own love toward us, in that while we were yet sinners, Christ died for us" (Romans 5:8).

- Agape initiates: It is on a mission. It follows the way of Christ. Don't wait for further orders. Start making a difference with your life. "This is love: not that we loved God, but that he loved us and sent his Son as an atoning sacrifice for our sins" (1 John 4:10 NIV).

- Agape is inspired: It is Spirit generated. Take the lid off. Get ready to receive a fresh pouring. Get ready to overflow. "The love of God has been poured out within our hearts through the Holy Spirit" (Romans 5:5).

- Agape is a learning curve: You're a refillable vessel. Bestow agape generously. You cannot plumb its expanse. Give and receive; sow and reap. Be a lifelong dispensary. "That you, being rooted and grounded in love, may be able to comprehend with all the saints what is the breadth and length and height and depth, and to know the love of Christ which surpasses knowledge, that you may be filled up to all the fullness of God" (Ephesians 3:17-19).

- Agape is our testimony: Love properly introduces God into every situation. It upsets the apple cart of expectations. Be different. Love haters. Be like your heavenly Father. "If you love those who love you, what reward do you have? Do not even the tax collectors do the same? If you greet only your brothers, what more are you doing than others?" (Matthew 5:46-47).

- Agape is spiritual intelligence: Earthly visibility is limited. The smelly haze of evil gets thick. One day the fog will lift. Know that Love is always shining down on you above the mist. "For now we see in a mirror dimly, but then face to face; now I know in part, but then I will know fully just as I also have been fully known" (1 Corinthians 13:12).

THE SUPREMACY AND SYMPTOMS OF LOVE

The church has long recognized the supreme role that Love plays in the spiritual life. Early church fathers declared, "Charity [Love] is the form of the virtues."[4] Paul took it further: "The greatest of these is love" (1 Corinthians 13:13). Love alone is eternal.[5] In heaven, Faith will no longer be required, and all Hopes will have been fulfilled. Love alone will remain as the reality and rule of heaven.

Love is an unsurpassed quality of character. It generates a host of virtuous behaviors that might be called Love symptoms. They validate the presence and the purity of Love.

It is easy to say, "I Love." But if you can't back up your claims with evidence, you are kidding yourself. "But whoever has the world's goods, and sees his brother in need and closes his heart against him, how does the love of God abide in him?" (1 John 3:17). Got Love? Prove it! Show it!

It does not take a genius to figure out that people who are unkind, unforgiving and uncompassionate have little Love. Figuring out someone's spiritual condition is just like diagnosing someone's physical condition. Look at the symptoms. Do you want to know how loving you are? What are your symptoms? Do they match the symptoms of Love in 1 Corinthians 13? If not, you have a Love problem.

HUMAN LOVE VERSUS AGAPE LOVE

Agape Love originates from God's character. "Every good thing given and every perfect gift is from above,

At SpiritualProgress.com the spiritual assessments translate the many Scriptures on Love into a series of questions. When you answer them honestly, it gives you an accurate measurement of your level of Love.

coming down from the Father of lights, with whom there is no variation or shifting shadow" (James 1:17). The words *every good thing* mean that God is the origin for all true virtue in the world.

You may take issue with this. Perhaps you have met some individuals who, you believe, are very good people in and of themselves. What you are observing is the goodness that God has placed in creatures who are made in his image. God is still the source.

But beware! Under the thin veneer of human goodness lurks a very dark side. As virtuous as someone might appear, the truth is, you can never trust a person's deepest motives. The Bible reveals, "The heart is more deceitful than all else and is desperately sick; who can understand it?" (Jeremiah 17:9).

With God there is no "variation or shifting shadow." There is no duplicity. There are no hidden motives. His character never changes. God alone is perfect Love.

Agape Love is unique and distinctive. It goes much further than any human love could ever go. Try to grasp this mind-boggling truth: "While we were enemies we were reconciled to God through the death of His Son" (Romans 5:10). I can easily picture myself jumping into a raging river and risking my life to save one of my children. I can't conceive doing the same to save a lifelong, intractable enemy.

Would you make the ultimate sacrifice for someone like that? That is exactly what God did for us in Christ. This contrast helps us to just begin to grasp the amazing span of God's agape Love!

A TRUE STORY OF FALSE LOVE

The father of the family, whom we shall call Dave, attended church faithfully. He was a prominent leader in the community and was highly regarded by many inside and outside of the church. He had made a financial killing through large military contracts and was very generous and considerate of the poor. He looked like the perfect Christian. He had been a major donor in the latest building program of the church.

There was another, less known, less likeable, side to Dave. He had fathered several children through a succession of newer, ever-younger and ever-prettier wives. It was also well-known by everyone in his family that he had recently fathered a child out of wedlock. Dave was a Christian, but his family was a mess.

The family consisted of a bizarre mix of half sisters and half brothers from different marriages living under one big roof. As if this weren't challenging enough, there was a toxic climate of blatant favoritism that originated from Dad. Personalities were warped as the children struggled for significance. Time would prove that their family was an effective breeding ground for every form of immoral and illegal behavior known to man. Their family was a disaster in the making.

Damon, the eldest son, had been spoiled from birth. Everyone knew he was Dad's favorite. Whatever he wanted, he got. His character greatly suffered for it. Damon had little capacity for self-control and none for self-denial. His character flaws, compliments of Dad, set the stage for a great family tragedy.

Damon fell in "love" with one of his half sisters, whom we'll call Tammy. Tammy was a committed Christian. She was probably the most emotionally well-balanced of all the kids and had strong moral values. She attended the church youth group every week and was passionate about serving God. She rebuffed every hint of interest that Damon displayed and tried to make light of it. Damon could not handle the rejection. He had convinced himself that he was "in love" with her. This was the first time in his young, selfish life that he desperately wanted something that he could not have. He became obsessed with Tammy and began stalking her. His unfulfilled desires occupied his mind, day and night.

One afternoon, Damon lured Tammy into his bedroom under a false pretense. He locked the door and tried to force the issue. He pled with her. He told her about his undying love for her. He begged. He had to have her. He began to force his way with her and when she resisted, he hungrily raped her.

She sobbed. His so-called love was exposed for what it was: hatred. Hate takes; Love gives.

The selfish hate that had always been his true motive surfaced with a vengeance. He berated Tammy. He unleashed a torrent of hurtful insults. He screamed for her to leave his room. He told her that he never wanted to see her again.

Tammy was devastated and ashamed. Not knowing what to do or who to talk to, she went to her full-blooded brother Adam and sobbed out the entire story. Adam was enraged.

Adam angrily marched off for a talk with Dad. He knew that Damon was Dad's favorite. He demanded justice for his sister. Dave, who was relatively fresh off his recent extramarital escapade, listened with shocked sorrow. He was angry with himself and furious at Damon. The more Dave thought about the situation, the more he felt trapped. How could he lecture anyone about morality? How could he punish someone for what he had done himself? His special love for Damon and his father's love for Tammy left him no easy choices. At this critical juncture Dave continued to choose the wrong path. It was a decision that his children would pay for the rest of their lives.

Dave's tragic story had begun with lies about Love. He had stolen another man's wife. The more he took, the more Love escaped him. Dave believed in lies. Damon had followed in his footsteps.

The family's tortured story made national news. If you want to read more about this family and discover their real names and circumstances, then I invite you to read 2 Samuel 13. Dave is King David of ancient Israel. Damon is Amnon. Tammy is Tamar, and Adam is Absalom. The story is not only true, but God felt it was important enough to include in the Bible.

REFLECTIONS

At first glance the story makes no sense. Tamar had not enticed Amnon. How can someone go from being madly in love to passionately hateful in an instant? The answer is simple: they cannot.

Amnon, like a lot of people, was confused about Love. His *feelings* of Love were nothing more than selfishness. It was taking, not giving. It was hatred in disguise. Hate puts its own desires and needs *above* those of another. It ignores the welfare of others. Love gives. It puts its own desires and needs *behind* the needs of others. This is the manner in which Christ loved us.

"Do nothing from selfishness or empty conceit, but with humility of mind regard one another as more important than yourselves; do not merely look out for your own personal interests, but also for the interests of others. Have this attitude in yourselves which was also in Christ Jesus" (Philippians 2:3-5). What attitude? The very same attitude that Christ had when he gave his very life for us on the cross! Maybe you're thinking, *You've got to be kidding me! That's not reasonable!*

You're right. It's Love. Jesus stated it plainly so we could not misunderstand his meaning: "A new commandment I give to you, that you love one another, even as I have loved you, that you also love one another" (John 13:34).

This seems like an impossibly high moral standard. Earlier Jesus had taught a more reasonable approach to Love, commonly known as the Golden Rule. "In everything, therefore, treat people the same way you want them to treat you" (Matthew 7:12). I think I might be able to muster up enough Love to treat people the way I want to be treated. But to Love others the way that *Christ* loved us? That's quite another matter. I definitely need an outside power source for that!

Why do so many marriages fail today? In many cases it is because human-based love does not *empower* people enough to give enough. When the going gets tough, they lack the motivational capacity to last for the long haul. The span of our love is too limited. We need the limitless capacity of God's Love. We can't be the husband or wife we want to be without the Motivational Virtue of Love at work in our lives.

Like Amnon, people commonly confuse lust with Love. Women end up mistrusting men. Men end up embittered by women. In many relationships, neither person has seen the real deal. They marry in lust (for the purposes of fulfilling their own needs), and fall out of lust (when their needs are not met). It's graciously labeled "irreconcilable differences." They divorce and continue their misguided search for Love. Anyone want to rate his or her chances for success in the next relationship?

SHOW ME THE LOVE

Prior to my accepting Christ as a teenager, a cute and vivacious Christian cheerleader from my high school handed me a booklet. It was the Gospel of Matthew in an easy-to-read translation. I was genuinely curious and wanted to impress the girl, so I began to read the booklet in earnest. I vividly recall my frustration when I got to the part about turning your cheek and loving your enemies.

I stopped reading and put the booklet down. I was discouraged. *That's not me!* I thought. *There is no way I can be a Christian.* One month later, when I invited Christ into my heart, I received an inner capacity to Love that was *not me*. It was far beyond anything I could have imagined. The letter of the Law, "Love your enemies," had fallen on the unfertile soil of a self-centered heart. The Spirit gave me a transformed life. I needed and got a new heart.

LOVE AND EMPATHY

Figure 11.1 illustrates that Love, at its core, is about giving and empathy. The concept of giving is widely understood. Empathy bears some explaining.

Empathy is the ability to truly place oneself in the position, feelings and perspectives of another. It is a remarkable spiritual capacity when exercised toward those who have grievously wronged us. God did it. Empathy has a profound grasp of human nature. It is living proof that people can overcome evil with compassion and forgiveness. Empathy rules over evil.

God, in Christ, put himself in your shoes. He knows your perspectives. He has felt your feelings. "He set aside the privileges of deity and took on the status of a slave, became human! Having become human, he stayed human. It was an incredibly humbling process" (Philippians 2:7-8 *The Message*).

God has empathy for every aspect of your life. No one knows you like Christ. No one better understands your temptations and struggles. "That's why he had to enter into every detail of human life. Then, when he came before God as high priest to get rid of the people's sins, he would have already experienced it all himself—all the pain, all the testing—and would be able to help where help was needed" (Hebrews 2:17-18 *The Message*).

SYMPTOMATIC VIRTUES

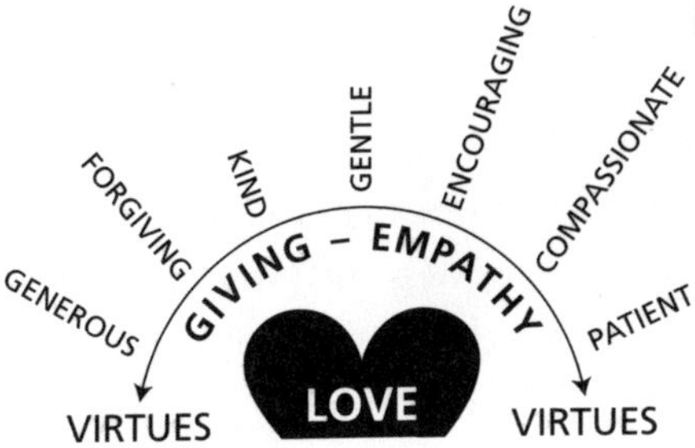

Figure 11.1

Figure 11.1 displays some of the key character traits of a Love-filled heart. Love, as we have seen with Faith and Hope, has specific attitudes and behaviors that are associated with it.

The Bible provides an inventory of Love symptoms. The list in figure 11.1 was distilled from an exhaustive search of the Scriptures. One example is found in Paul's words to the church at Ephesus: "With all humility and gentleness, with patience, showing tolerance for one another in love" (Ephesians 4:2). Paul added more symptoms in his letter to the Colossian church: "Put on a heart of compassion, kindness, humility, gentleness and patience; bearing with one another, and forgiving each other. . . . Beyond all these things put on love" (Colossians 3:12-14).

Love might best be defined as a character condition that cares deeply for people and generates an excessive and unflappable spirit of generosity. You learn early in life that there are two kinds of people—givers and takers. We are all born takers. We cry and scream and demand our way into life. Wise parents pop the self-deity bubble early.

No matter how great our parents were, our nature remains fundamentally selfish. We cannot decide, in our own strength, to become genuine serial givers. We can't sustain it. We need to be empowered by the Motivational Virtue of Love.

THE LOVE CONTINUUM

Love is not a fixed point. It is a zone, as illustrated in figure 11.2. Motivational forces exist that would either diminish Love or hype it into a false form of Love. Unresolved anger and selfishness open the door to negative motivational forces that would diminish Love. These are the takers. Emotional neediness and possessiveness open the door to negative motivational forces that would hype Love. These personality types could be labeled the controllers.

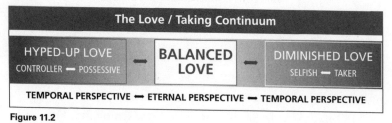

Figure 11.2

Figure 11.2 illustrates the two imbalances that lie on either side of authentic Love. It is similar to the power zone graphic in chapter four, but focuses solely on Love. Everyone understands how Love becomes diminished. Hyped-up Love is less obvious because it can look like Love to the uninformed. This imbalance is characterized by emotional control and possessiveness. These imbalances will be described in much greater detail in the next chapter.

FALSE GIVING

Giving is at the center of authentic Love. "For God so loved the world, that He gave His only begotten Son" (John 3:16). God's Love is measured by the level of his generosity. We need to understand authentic giving if we are to avoid Love's counterfeits.

"Mary is the most loving person I know," her friends exclaim. "She always thinks of everyone else and puts the needs of others ahead of her own. She is such a giver!"

Someone with discernment may look at Mary and come to a completely different conclusion. "Mary gives but there are always strings attached. She oversteps personal boundaries. The expectations she puts on others are suffocating. Whatever Mary's condition, it certainly is not Love."

Giving and self-deception can go hand in hand. The motives behind giving can be very confusing. That's why Jesus gave such detailed instructions for how we give. "But when you give to the poor, do not let your left hand know what your right hand is doing, so that your giving will be in secret; and your Father who sees what is done in secret will reward you" (Matthew 6:3-4).

The most telling verse in the Bible about the practice of false giving can be found in the words of Paul. "If I give all I possess to the poor and surrender my body to the flames, but have not love, I gain nothing" (1 Corinthians 13:3 NIV 1984). This is a highly provocative thought. Even the ultimate sacrifice of dying for another can be a pointless, cleverly concealed form of self-love.

Never try to prove your Love through giving. Love can't be emulated or faked. Love effortlessly validates itself and is far too strong to contain. When you spend enough time basking in the energy of God's Love, Love-giving will naturally flow out of your life.

THE FIELD OF CONTENTION FOR LOVE

Figure 11.3 shows the full spectrum of character traits that are associated with Love or the lack of it. The Motivational Virtue of Love is positioned against the Motivational Evil of the lust of the flesh. The image of a divided heart shows that, in many ways, Love and the lust of the flesh are opposites of one another. Love is about giving. The lust of the flesh is all about taking.

These opposing motivations, as you can see, produce very different personality traits and behaviors in people. One leads to compassion

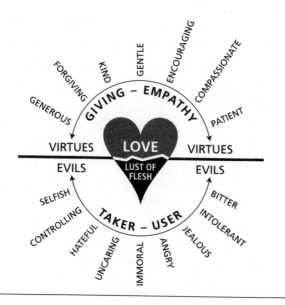

Figure 11.3

and the other to jealousy. One is generous and forgiving while the other is hateful and intolerant. One is patient and kind while the other is an angry controller.

Which kind of person would you prefer to hang out with? Lust-of-the-flesh personality types are attracted to people who meet their needs. They are selfish and controlling. Love-filled people care about you. They are kind and generous friends.

The Motivational Virtue of Love and the Motivational Evil of the lust of the flesh compete for dominion over your heart. The lust of the flesh pulls you in the direction of self-fulfillment. Love pulls you in the direction of fulfilling the needs of others. As with Faith and Hope, the motivation that you feed the most is the one that wins the most.

Do you struggle with resentment? Are you compassionate or hard-hearted toward others? The answers to these and other symptomatic questions help you to quickly zero in on your growth areas. Figure 11.3 provides a simple visual model to help you note your strengths and growth areas of Love. Honest and accurate examination is the key to staying on track in the pursuit of your personal growth objectives.

FINAL THOUGHTS

The Motivational Virtue of Love makes a visible impact on a person's character. Agape Love bursts at the seams to find expression. Love loves to give. It takes the initiative, even in the face of evil. Had God waited for humankind to come to him, he would still be waiting. Love breaks the gridlock of evil. It does not wait for apologies or changed attitudes before it acts.

The church is singularly qualified to speak to the world's confusion about Love. God is Love. It is impossible to lift up Christ without elevating his Love. He is the definition and the source of Love.

Forget about embarking on a quest to act more loving. Love symptoms are too hard to fake for very long. Embrace the Motivational Virtue of Love. Walk in the contexts of the Spirit, the Word and community where God can speak to you about Love. Practice the spiritual disciplines that were detailed in chapter six. Let God pour agape Love into your soul. It will define your character and change everything about your life.

12

THE DISTORTIONS OF LOVE
Love Imbalances and the Power Zone

> *I have found the paradox, that if you love until it hurts,*
> *there can be no more hurt, only more love.*
>
> Mother Teresa

> *If someone says, "I love God,"*
> *and hates his brother, he is a liar;*
> *for the one who does not love his brother*
> *whom he has seen, cannot love God*
> *whom he has not seen.*
>
> 1 John 4:20

Love is the most emotionally powerful of the Motivational Virtues. Passions can be tricky to navigate. They are volatile. Fervent feelings make it easy to lose one's normal composure. This is why even small imbalances in the Motivational Virtue of Love can swiftly lead to damaging behaviors with consequences far beyond one's intentions.

We have seen how each of the Motivational Virtues plays a different role in making spiritual progress. Faith can be more cerebral.

Hope is the most stoic. And Love is the most powerfully passionate. Let's explore how these passions can go awry.

IMBALANCED LOVE

Diminished and hyped Love makes people susceptible to highly charged emotions. Anger, hatred, jealousy and envy are strong feelings that are the result of imbalanced Love. These passions are unstable and can quickly escalate into a whirlwind of troubles. Their propensity for damage gives rise to a legal term: *crimes of passion.*

Solomon, with all of his wisdom, knew that imbalanced Love was not something to be trifled with. It was as dangerous over three thousand years ago as it is today.

> Love is as strong as death,
> Jealousy is as severe as Sheol;
> Its flashes are flashes of fire,
> The very flame of the LORD. (Song of Solomon 8:6)

The fiery love that Solomon describes is not to be confused with agape Love. Agape is balanced Love, as described in the previous chapter. It is the most stable substance in the universe. Balanced Love "does not seek its own" (1 Corinthians 13:5). Love puts the needs of others ahead of its own interests. Envy and jealousy have no elbowroom when agape Love is present. Balanced Love naturally thinks and behaves the way Paul encouraged us to live: "Make my joy complete by being of the same mind, maintaining the same love. . . . With humility of mind regard one another as more important than yourselves; do not merely look out for your own personal interests, but also for the interests of others" (Philippians 2:2-4).

Wouldn't the world be a different place if everyone acted this way!

LIFE IN THE SPIRIT

Agape Love contradicts human nature. It is otherworldly. How do we acquire this spiritual Love? It comes from associating with the Spirit. God is the only source who can breathe this kind of Love into our hearts. What does hanging out with the Spirit look like? Paul described the character-transforming nature of Spirit encounters: "Now the Lord is the Spirit, and where the Spirit of the Lord is, there is liberty. But we all, with unveiled face, beholding as in a mirror the glory of the Lord, are being transformed into the same image from glory to glory, just as from the Lord, the Spirit" (2 Corinthians 3:17-18).

Notice the words *But we all.* This is not some special experience intended for super religious people. This is meant to be the universal, ongoing experience of ordinary Christ followers.

Christ, through his sacrificial death on the cross, has removed our sins, guilt and shame. God's Love has bridged the impenetrable chasm between himself and humankind. A great many stand inside the gates of God's forgiveness and progress no further. They hold a waiting vigil until Christ returns but never move into a lifestyle of walking with the Spirit.

Faith ushers us into the spiritual life. Don't stop now! What is the next destination? We must learn to live in his presence. The Spirit transports us there. Once there, something amazing happens. The Bible says we enter into a process where we "are being transformed into the same image." What image? God's image! We behold "the glory of the Lord." Get the point? It is impossible to see God and not be changed! God is Love. Time with God changes us into loving beings. We supernaturally become Love. Don't expect to totally understand it; just experience it.

Every other inspirational source for Love is inadequate. You may pledge undying Love to the person of your dreams, but it will not transform your core nature. You may Love your family and be willing to die for them, but what is the span of your Love? How do you feel about the rest of the world?

Human love is but a shadow of God's Love. God's Love is heavenly. It's also earthly. For Love, Jesus bore the dust of the earth by taking on human flesh.

THE FLESH AND SPIRIT AT WAR

If we are to make spiritual progress in Love we need to understand the severe differences between life in the Spirit and life in the flesh. They have mutually exclusive agendas. Which one will define you? The spiritual life won't win without regular investments. Paul urged an active spiritual lifestyle. We need to take regular walks with the Spirit. "But I say, walk by the Spirit, and you will not carry out the desire of the flesh. For the flesh sets its desire against the Spirit, and the Spirit against the flesh; for these are in opposition to one another" (Galatians 5:16-17).

Agape Love is the work of the Spirit. Imbalanced Love is the work of the flesh. The Spirit is stronger than the flesh, as we just read in Galatians 5:16: "Walk by the Spirit . . . you will *not* carry out the desire of the flesh."

What is the desire of the flesh? Paul gives us a lovely list to contemplate: "Now the deeds of the flesh are evident, which are: immorality, impurity, sensuality, idolatry, sorcery, enmities, strife, jealousy, outbursts of anger, disputes, dissensions, factions, envying, drunkenness, carousing, and things like these" (Galatians 5:19-21). When I look at this passage, it appears to be a complete anti-agape Love list. Look how emotionally charged the flesh is! It strikes me that the motivational outcomes from this list could be responsible for close to 100 percent of all crimes ever committed.

Love is something we have to get right. The quality of our life and the lives of those around us depend on it. Love is a major component of our character. It is impossible to embrace our potential as human beings without it.

FALSE LOVE

It is easy to advertise, "I Love." People say it all the time. But this is not a statement that should be made casually. Love is a profound condition and a remarkable commitment of the heart. Don't overstate it! This form of hypocrisy hurts and alienates people.

Fortunately, there is a way to biblically assess the measure of our Love. This is great news! We need a way to be honest with ourselves. It's something that does not come easily to us. We all have an amazing capacity for self-deception. Validation is a big deal, especially for conscientious Christians. Nothing has done more to hurt the cause of Christ over the centuries than bad-acting, unloving Christians.

Why do so many people overrepresent their Love for God? Love is priceless and people always try to counterfeit really valuable things. Sometimes it's because people know just how unloving they really are and they fear discovery. Others act in insincere ways to be accepted in the midst of religious peer pressure. Still others believe they Love God when all the evidence points to the contrary.

The incongruity between what Christians say and what they do has created a great deal of cynicism in the world. Mark Twain articulated it with his usual cutting wit: "There has been only one Christian. They caught him and crucified him—early."[1] He went on to make the cynical observation, "If Christ were here there is one thing he would not be—a Christian." Twain speaks for multitudes of skeptics who are waiting to see evidence of genuine Love.

THE LOVING PERSONA

The balanced graphic for Love is just like the balanced graphics used in previous chapters to depict Faith and Hope.

The loving persona represents someone who has *both* a passionate devotion to God *and* a passionate desire to make a difference in people's lives. It is their genuine Love for people that validates the purity of their Love for God. Remove this critical evidence of Love and it is false Love. Love, like every Motivational Virtue, is validated through the caliber of our relationships.

Relating to God. Possessing a fervent Love for God is the first and greatest commandment: "You shall love the Lord your God with all your heart, and with all your soul, and with all your mind, and with all your strength" (Mark 12:30). Nothing is more character defining than having a passionate Love for God. It motivates a world of goodness.

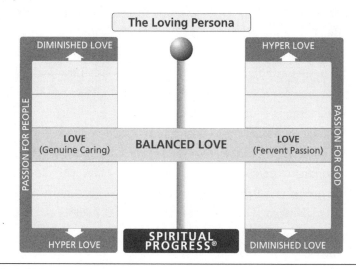

Figure 12.1

Loving someone with "*all* your heart" sounds like the lyrics to a great romantic song. It actually is the greatest love song in history. Did you know that God sings love songs over his children? Have you ever thought of your Creator in that way? Hear God's Love rising from the pages of the Bible: "He will take great delight in you; in his love he . . . will rejoice over you with singing" (Zephaniah 3:17 NIV). Once we start to picture God in this way, our lives change. God is no longer a cosmic tough guy. His tender Love melts our hearts.

Relating to people. Now we come to the proof of Love. It is easy to say, "I love God." God is invisible, but the way we relate to people is highly observable. Loving God without loving people is impossible. It is inhumane Love. Does that even sound feasible? Yet it describes the condition of a great many people. Let's make sure that we hear the truth loud and clear: "If someone says, 'I love God,' and hates his brother, he is a liar; for the one who does not love his brother whom he has seen, cannot love God whom he has not seen" (1 John 4:20).

The evidence is in. It is *impossible* to love God without loving people. The authenticity and depth of our love for God can be accurately "measured" by the caliber of our love for people. This capacity to quantify something as subjective as our Love for God is huge. It provides reliable metrics that can be used to assess the most important aspect of our character.

What kinds of relationships surround you? Is your life filled with loving friends? Do you seem to be regularly at odds with people? Are you largely isolated? Are you disillusioned and withdrawn due to past negative relationships? Are you licking your wounds, resentful and angry? The answers to these kinds of questions provide a clear window into how much you have allowed God's Love to fill your heart.

THE UNCONNECTED PERSONA

The unconnected persona is the picture of what happens when one's Love begins to become diminished. Diminished Love impacts the way we relate to God and to people. There are two traits that define the character tendencies of the unconnected Christian. They are essentially two sides of the same coin.

1. Isolation from God: This is the result of self-absorption or blaming God.

2. Isolation from People: This is the result of self-absorption or blaming people.

Diminished Love becomes a "form" of Christianity that relies more on the momentum of habits than fire in the engine room. Gone is the zeal and enthusiastic character of the new convert. Compassion for others has taken a backseat. An unconnected soul is now at the steering wheel. Collisions are in your future.

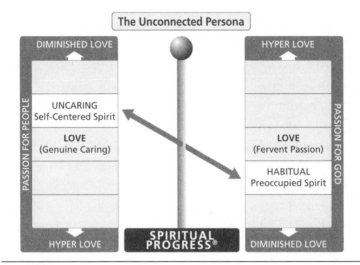

Figure 12.2

Love for God. I vividly recall the first morning I awakened after accepting Christ. His loving presence instantly surrounded me. A smile was plastered on my face to the extent that my sister asked me what was wrong with me as I drove her to our high school that morning. She thought I was on drugs.

Nothing was more important, in those early days, than sustaining the sense of Christ's presence in my life. I was dependent on it like a baby with a bottle. I went to five Bible studies a week in addition to attending church every time the doors were open. One long-term Christian, who was a leader in the church, told me one day that I would "calm down" after I had more time as a Christian. I was offended. "Calming down" seemed synonymous with embalming fluid.

I was on fire for Christ in Southern California in 1971, which was a hotbed of one of the great revivals of the church. I was disturbed by the lack of evident passion in the hearts of many of the people in the church. My judgmental spirit was a part of my spiritual immaturity.

Over time, I came to understand some of the truth of some of the elder Christian's words. My old sinful nature was not dead. It had just been overshadowed for a time by God's protective glory over a spiritual newborn. In time I began to hear the clamor of the world and its lusts. Sin waged its unrelenting war against my heart. I grew to have far more compassion on those whose passion for God had withered. I determined to remain passionate in my relationship with God, a battle I have fought with varying success over the years. It is a lifelong pursuit.

Relating to God. Jesus spoke some hard-hitting words to the church at Ephesus that are very relevant today: "But I have this against you, that you have left your first love" (Revelation 2:4). Anyone who is married knows that it takes work to keep the flames of Love burning hot. The Bible describes the unloving character of people in the last days: "For men will be lovers of self . . . rather than lovers of God, holding to a form of godliness, although they have denied its power; Avoid such men as these" (2 Timothy 3:2, 4-5).

God has some steep competition for our affections in these self-centered times. We need to fully meet and embrace God's Love. It is a gift from God. When we Love God it is not some amazing and wondrous thing that *we* are doing. "We love, because He first loved us" (1 John 4:19). All good things come from God—even our Love for God.

Relating to people. It's easy to be deceived about our level of Love for others. Our actions and language betray us. Self-justifications take many forms. We try to isolate unloving relationships as special cases. It's not *my* character issue. *They* have a problem. These futile attempts to absolve ourselves from the responsibility to love our neighbor give rise to some ridiculous statements.

"I love them, I just don't like them."

"I love them, I just choose not to associate with them."

"I love them, I just can't trust them."

Ask yourself a simple question. Where would you and I be if God loved that way? Let's recall the way that God loves people: "While we were enemies we were reconciled to God through the death of His Son" (Romans 5:10); and "This is love: not that we loved God, but that he loved us and sent his Son as an atoning sacrifice for our sins" (1 John 4:10 NIV).

Distancing ourselves from taking any responsibility for difficult or strained relationships should serve as a warning sign for us. This often happens with family relationships where unresolved pain can go all the way back to one's childhood. Love is strong enough to reach across many decades and heal our souls.

There is an unloving attitude that has reached epic proportions in our modern times. It expresses itself in words like this: "If they don't like it, then it is their problem, not mine." Contrast this with the Bible's perspective on Love: "For if because of food your brother is hurt, you are no longer walking according to love. Do not destroy with your food him for whom Christ died" (Romans 14:15). Food, in this case, meant eating food that had been offered to idols. The food was perfectly good, but the effects of eating it were not. It violated the sensitivities of many people during the time of Christ. You can replace the word *food* with anything. The principle of Love teaches us to put the needs of others ahead of our own desires, as Paul did. "With humility of mind regard one another as more important than yourselves; do not merely look out for your own personal interests, but also for the interests of others" (Philippians 2:3-4).

Authentic Love reaches out. It initiates. It engages. "But whoever has the world's goods, and sees his brother in need and closes his heart against him, how does the love of God abide in him?" (1 John 3:17). Withdrawal from social responsibility is clear evidence of a character deficiency in the area of Love.

The unconnected persona is someone who has become relationally isolated in some area of his or her life. One of the biggest causes of separation is tied to a decision not to forgive someone. Most people do not fully understand the impact on their character when they blame others. Jesus taught a startling truth: "But if you do not forgive others, then your Father will not forgive your transgressions" (Matthew 6:15).

Why such a hard stance? When people wrong us, they have done nothing more to us than we have done to God on countless occasions. We incur judgment on ourselves when we choose to not forgive someone. We put the development of our character on hold. Unresolved hurt makes us serve time for someone else's crime. How smart is that? Love is spiritual intelligence. Now we know why Love and forgiveness are such a big deal to God. He wants us to live free from the forces of evil.

THE INTOLERANT PERSONA

The intolerant persona illustrates what happens when Love goes from somewhat diminished to substantially diminished. It's a very unfriendly place. It makes few allowances for anyone, including one's self. It is a lonely and grumpy condition of the soul. The uncaring and selfish traits of the unconnected persona have become more pronounced. In its most advanced "Christian" stage, it hides an outright hatred of others behind the mask of phony religious posturing. It's a most unimpressive façade to the world.

Relating to God. Isolation has a devastating impact on one's relationship with God. When people isolate themselves, for whatever reason, they increase their vulnerability to evil. Self-deception has not only moved in, but it has taken over the house. The occupant is comfortable and unaware of their perilous plight.

This is problematic for those who used to have a warm, authentic relationship with God. The spiritual life does not operate well in memory mode. The spiritual joys of yesterday are quickly forgotten. The searing truths of God's Word quickly lose their relevance in a rapidly growing tangle of demonic lies.

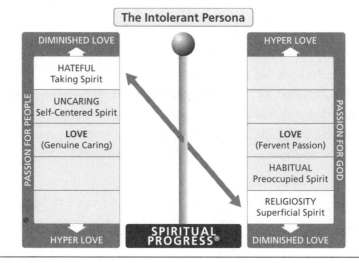

Figure 12.3

God encounters are like the manna that sustained the ancient Israelites in the desert. Spiritual health requires a daily dose. Jesus said, "I am the bread of life; he who comes to Me will not hunger" (John 6:35). Stale bread has little nutritional value for the soul. In the absence of fresh encounters, false perceptions of God linger and grow. Weakened Love grows weaker. The seeds of hatred grow and dominate the landscape.

The intolerant persona has the bent of a rigid personality devoid of compassion. This is similar to the spiritual condition of the Pharisees during the time of Christ. Jesus condemned their false Love. Their fixation on the external trappings of religion in their attempts to *appear* holy brought his sharp rebuke. Jesus called them white-washed tombs that were pretty on the outside but a rotten mess of dead men's bones on the inside (see Matthew 23:27). Love goes deeper than a paint job.

Like heavenly bureaucrats, the intolerant persona can quote chapter and verse. You can plead your case, but you know bureaucrats. It is like trying to explain your case to a stony-faced employee at the Department of Motor Vehicles. There is no room for mercy. They have the "rules" memorized and are incapable of painting outside the lines. No mercy for you.

A Jesus story: An "official" religious spirit. This brings us to a poignant story that involved Jesus and the intolerant officials of his day. It exposed the utterly loveless nature of their religion. They possessed a form of godliness that was utterly devoid of care and Love for people.

> And He was teaching in one of the synagogues on the Sabbath. And there was a woman who for eighteen years had had a sickness caused by a spirit; and she was bent double, and could not straighten up at all. When Jesus saw her, He called her over and said to her, "Woman, you are freed from your sickness." And He laid His hands on her; and immediately she was made erect again and began glorifying God. But the synagogue official, indignant because Jesus had healed on the Sabbath, began saying to the crowd in response, "There are six days in which work should be done; so come during them and get healed, and not on the Sabbath day." (Luke 13:10-14)

There is no doubt that the synagogue official was regarded as a very "spiritual" man by most of his flock. Legalistic piety is often confused with true spirituality. Little did he realize that his lack of compassion for people exposed his lack of Love for God.

Religion is the enemy of humanity. It replaces Love with laws and relationships with regulations. Christianity, at its authentic core, is a Love relationship with a loving God in the midst of a loving community. The synagogue official was so mired in legalism that he was blinded to a most amazing manifestation of God's Love in his own church.

Consider the woman's pitiful plight. God's house should have been filled with joy that day. It speaks volumes that the official could not be happy for her.

THE NEEDY PERSONA

The needy persona is the picture of what happens when one's Love begins to become hyped up. This Love imbalance heads in the opposite direction of diminished Love. Hyper Love takes authentic Love and morphs it into an unhealthy form of emotionalism. This impacts the way we relate to God and to people. Left untreated, the needy persona (somewhat hyped-up Love) can progress and take on more of the extreme personality traits of the demanding persona (described in the next section).

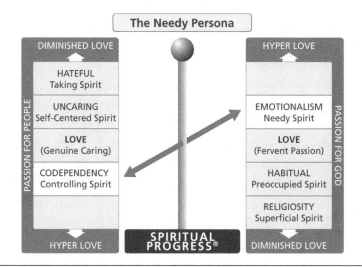

Figure 12.4

Relating to God. Nothing builds a stronger sense of personal confidence and security than receiving and growing in the unconditional Love of God. God's Love is based on historical fact. He took on the form of man, suffered and died for you in the person of Christ. Subsequent to that, Jesus made some long-term commitments to his children. Here is one great example: "He Himself has said, 'I will never desert you, nor will I ever forsake you'" (Hebrews 13:5).

The needy persona lets feelings, rather than facts, serve as their guiding light. One's spiritual welfare becomes a highly subjective matter. This over-reliance on one's emotional state creates character instabilities.

Emotionalism trumps God's Word with fickle feelings. Divine promises are crushed at the feet of moodiness. The needy persona feels blessed by God one day and forlorn the next. This character imbalance profoundly impacts one's relationships with people.

Relating to people. The needy persona is the result of unresolved personal insecurities. This deficiency creates an unhealthy dependency on others. Dependent character types are either vulnerable to, or the culprits behind, the manipulation of others. Imbalanced Love creates unhealthy relationships.

Two relational dynamics emerge. It takes a partnership of neediness to sustain a codependent relationship. There are two parties on the dance floor—the *controlee* and the *controller*. Insecurities drive dysfunctional behaviors from both sides of a relationship.

Needy people may look like caring, giving individuals. They use acts of kindness, gifts, words of praise, personal emotional crises and many other means to entangle unwary souls in a web of dependency. The reality is that each side in the bargain tries to take more than they give. This is not a recipe for strong enduring relationships.

Balanced Love relates to others with a healthy dynamic of mutuality, meaning that each person, over the long haul, equally invests in and gives to the needs of the other. In balanced Love, each side in the bargain tries to give more than they take. This is a good recipe for strong enduring relationships.

The words of Jesus are insightful: "You shall love your neighbor as yourself" (Matthew 19:19). *Self-Love* is the foundation upon which all healthy relationships are built. Personal security empowers people to be an unconditional giver to others. Strong self-Love is the result of growing in our awareness of God's unconditional Love for us. I love the apostle Paul's prayer: "That you, being rooted and grounded in love, may be able to comprehend with all the saints what is the breadth and length and height and depth, and to know the love of Christ which surpasses knowledge, that you may be filled up to all the fullness of God" (Ephesians 3:17-19). "Filled up" people are not defined by neediness. They make the greatest of friends.

THE DEMANDING PERSONA

The demanding persona is a picture of what happens when one's Love has become more intensely hyped up. This is an amplified version of the worst traits of the needy persona. Their heightened imbalances have a huge impact on the way they relate to God and to people. This persona suffers from deeply unresolved insecurities. Life is *all* about how they *feel*. Get ready for a rocky ride!

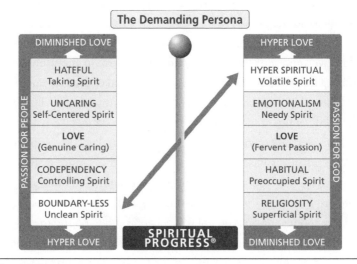

Figure 12.5

Relating to God. The demanding persona has a heightened sense of neediness due to their great relational distance from God. Only God's Love can fill the void and calm their souls. Their extreme disquiet generates extreme emotions and behaviors. Human nature abhors an imbalance. Neediness must be compensated for. Demanding personas offset their inner insecurities with emotive religious fervor. To the uninformed, they look to be very close to God.

What sad irony! They already have what they most desperately need. God loves them unconditionally. Their insecurities stiff-arm heaven's embrace. The very thing they need, they reject.

We all desperately need his touch. Spiritual isolation withers the soul. It generates insecurities at the deepest levels of our beings. The demanding persona, driven by its desperate inner neediness, charges full speed ahead.

Relating to people. God created us to be spiritually connected to him. Nothing else can fill this void. When there is no intimacy with God, our primal relationship, it has a huge impact on every other relationship. Spiritual neediness is never a good starting point for any relationship.

Demanding personas are emotions based. Consequently, they often overrepresent their connection with God, to themselves and others. Crazy things happen once someone makes the leap and starts to believe that their own feelings represent spiritual truth. "Thus says the Lord" is the coinage of their realm. Who dares take issue with such passionate convictions? They are modern-day false prophets.

When truth is based on how you feel, God becomes a subset of your emotions. God is entirely under your control. "Thus says the Lord" is, in reality, "These are my feelings." You become God.

Demanding personas do not respect appropriate boundaries. They *feel* they have the spiritual depth to meddle in the lives of other people. After all, they are speaking for God! Their overreaching behaviors combined with their severe inner neediness are a toxic mix. It sets the stage for shocking sexual immorality.

The exposure of the sexual sin of spiritual leaders shocks the public. They appeared to have such an inspiring passion for God. How could such a thing have happened? The truth is that they had been struggling with major areas of insecurity and spiritual blindness. The absence of genuine Love made them highly vulnerable to the forces of evil.

An aggravating story of hyper Love. A pastor friend of mine told me how he was once confronted by one of these "false prophet" character types. They had just begun a large building program when a prominent man in their congregation made an appointment to see him. Seated in the pastor's office, he made a bold proclamation. "Thus says the Lord, you shall not build this building!" My friend, a wise and seasoned pastor, paused a moment before responding. "Well, brother," he calmly replied, "the concrete has been poured." I love his practical response to "super spiritual" nonsense. They had, in fact, just finished pouring the footings that morning. The church went forward and enjoyed a great season of growth in spite of the "prophet's" dire warnings.

As a pastor, I have seen and dealt with many of these over-spiritualized individuals through the years. It is never easy. They "hear from God." What could a pastor possibly need to say to them?

A creepy story of hyper Love. It felt creepy as Ron slowly worked his way in my direction. I dreaded the moment when he would arrive in front of me. He prayed in a loud, emotionally laden voice. He had a towel draped over his shoulder as he washed the feet of a pastor two seats down from me. Ron pled with God to forgive him for speaking ill of his pastors. His tears of repentance mixed with the warm water in his big, stainless-steel bowl.

The show began when Ron had approached our senior pastor with a "heartfelt" confession. He admitted to gossiping and speaking ill of the pastoral staff and felt he owed them all an apology. Then he made an unusual request. "Pastor, my sin has grieved God. I feel a part of my repentance requires me to wash the feet of all the pastoral staff." The senior pastor was a kind and gracious man. I am sure he did not know what to do with such a request.

Now I sat barefoot next to my colleagues in ministry. Something felt out of balance. I was squirming inside. I began to doubt myself. Maybe it was my problem. Was this a matter of my personal pride? I was a youth pastor at the beginning of my ministry. What did I know? So I sat there and decided to humble myself and graciously accept his act of repentance.

Two weeks later we found out that Ron had been having multiple, long-term affairs with women in the church. What hypocrisy! People were shocked. Others struggled. How could such an outwardly spiritual man with such a demonstrative "passion" for God have done such things?

FINAL THOUGHTS

Over three subsequent decades as a pastor, I have observed an unmistakable pattern. People who are the most passionately spiritual often have problems with dark passions. Individuals with this type of character malformation live in the land of feelings. That's why they are so easily deceived.

We have all witnessed the public and terrible tragedies of some televangelists and high-profile pastors in recent years. It seems that many of those who preached the hardest against sin were the greatest participants and victims of it. Were they all hypocrites? I think not. Is there something deeper afoot? I suspect so. I believe the culprit is a character flaw that was not addressed in a timely fashion.

How can such horrible failures be averted, or at least minimized? Churches need to become far more aware of the spiritual imbalances that eventually develop into such toxic personas. Character imbalances are most easily addressed early on. God's people need to have their eyes more widely opened to the symptoms of spiritual malaise and spiritual health. There is a pressing need for a biblically accurate spiritual assessment. The next chapter offers one. We need concrete answers that explain why we do what we do.

13

GROWING FORWARD

Assess, Discover and Grow

> *No one remains quite what he was
> when he recognizes himself.*
>
> Thomas Mann

> *And you will know the truth,
> and the truth will make you free.*
>
> John 8:32

This book began by describing the behavioral supply chain that exists behind our behaviors. Throughout we have asked and worked to answer the principal question, "Why do I do what I do?" This journey has led us to explore the positive and negative motivational forces that compete for and determine the nature of our character.

Faith, Hope and Love are the primary, positive motivational conditions of the heart. They are soul-nourishing fountains of virtue. Each one generates a highly specific and predictable pattern of character traits. There is always a reason behind why I do what I do. These associated *symptoms* make it possible to develop an accurate spiritual assessment. My character traits reveal my underlying motivations. Understanding my motivations is important because this is the realm of the Spirit and the focal point for the activity of God.

We have also explored the large biblical body of evidence behind the three primal, dark motivations that work to influence our behaviors and shape our character. The apostle John exposed them from the wizened perspective of old age. The lust of the flesh—hedonism—is a consuming, taking motivation that works against the giving motivation of true Love. The lust of the eyes—materialism—is fixated on that which is seen and works against the trusting motivation of Faith. The pride of life—egotism—struggles to find personal significance in this life and works against the optimistic, eternally secure motivation of Hope. We saw how these evil motivations began in the hearts of Adam and Eve when they succumbed to the original temptation and were the same ones that Christ overcame during his desert temptation.

The stage of moral, motivational conflict has been set. These six primary motivations, three virtuous and three evil, are the main arena where God is at work to grow and transform our hearts. Here we make expansive spiritual progress or suffer character-withering defeat. Are there other areas outside of this arena where God works? No doubt. But certainly we will do well in making spiritual progress if we focus on our basic motivations and grow in Faith, Hope and Love.

THE BIBLICAL CALL TO ASSESS OURSELVES

Spiritual life is a journey. We need to recognize that our motivations are subject to change. This is good news and bad news. Our character can improve but it can also worsen. Spirituality is far from a static state. Given this potential for change, we need a way to stay on track.

There is a biblical principle that helps us here. Paul advocated it: "Let a man [thoroughly] examine himself. . . . For if we searchingly examined ourselves [detecting our shortcomings and recognizing our own condition], we should not be judged" (1 Corinthians 11:28, 31 Amplified Bible). We need the ability to regularly and accurately assess ourselves. As you will see in the following pages, Jesus practiced it in his efforts to grow people. We need the truth about ourselves.

It is impossible to make spiritual progress without fresh spiritual insight. The Bible places personal insight high on the list of "must haves"—"Those who have insight will shine brightly like the brightness of the expanse of heaven, and those who lead the many to righteousness, like the stars forever and ever" (Daniel 12:3). The path to effective evangelism runs fastest in the light of good character.

THE MAKINGS OF A SPIRITUAL ASSESSMENT

How would one go about putting together a spiritual assessment? This is not to be confused with a spiritual gift assessment. Character is always far more important than gifts in God's kingdom. Good character guarantees a long, useful life of service to God. The starting point for a spiritual assessment is understanding a unique property of the Bible. It is a mirror, showing us something about ourselves.

There are large groupings of Scriptures that show us how we look in the area of Faith. The same is true about Hope and Love. When these groupings of Scripture verses are all gathered in one place, they have the power to give us a more comprehensive picture of ourselves.

Think of the combined light of a great many individual mirrors aimed at your heart. The result is an intensely focused beam of light that penetrates your soul. This is precisely the effect of a pastor's sermon that brings several passages together to make a bigger impact of truth. The key difference is that an assessment can be far more comprehensive in its scope than is possible in a sermon. When you put the scriptural spotlights of Faith, Hope and Love together, one clear image appears. It is your character.

Understanding the illumining power of God's Word, I began a

quest to bring the light of a great many Scriptures together into a single focus. I cataloged all of these character traits from the Bible on good and evil and sorted them based on frequency and intensity. I then distilled them into a list of top traits for each category. Finally, I crafted a series of simple questions that empower a person to make practical responses to the light of Scripture. You indicate how much a character trait applies or does not apply to your life.

This is the basis for the patented online character assessments at SpiritualProgress.com. When you answer the questions honestly, you are actually responding to a huge, widespread number of Scriptures in the Bible. Taking an assessment allows one to see a new, comprehensive and biblically penetrating view of one's self. Hundreds of early users in our pilot churches describe the assessments at Spiritual Progress.com as highly accurate and life changing.

THE VALUE OF SPIRITUAL ASSESSMENT

What's the value of having an assessment if you have nowhere to go with it? Below are some concrete steps you can take once you have an accurate spiritual assessment.

Step one: A diagnosis. Before we head out on our spiritual journey in earnest, we need to know our starting point. Where am I? We have to get our bearings. What do the Scriptures tell me about myself? What are my strengths and growth areas? Do I have any spiritual imbalance tendencies that I need to watch out for?

Step two: A prognosis. Once I have a handle on my general spiritual location, it is then possible to predict outcomes. What spiritual consequences and dysfunctions will I encounter if I remain on my present course? Without treatment, where am I headed? A bad prognosis can be the wakeup call that many people need to address their issues.

Step three: An effective growth plan. Finally, an accurate spiritual assessment provides the information needed to plot our course for maximum progress. What practical steps do I need to take? One might call this a spiritual treatment regimen. What specific messages and disciplines will give me the quickest gains in my greatest growth areas?

THE DIFFERENCES BETWEEN CHURCHES

If an individual can take a spiritual assessment, then so can a church. Churches have personalities and spiritual character traits that are very much like individuals. The reasons for this are obvious. People in a given church are under a specific leadership style that projects certain values and priorities. A congregation is largely moving through the same teaching track in the Bible. Corporate attitudes toward service, study, relationships and outreach have a profound effect on the spiritual makeup of individuals within a congregation. A church's DNA is merely a collective reflection of a critical mass of the spiritual traits of its leaders and adherents.

Some churches are very *sanguine*. They are warm, fuzzy places to belong. They can be very strong in relational love but weak in practical expressions of service. Other churches are totally into missions and outreach and "getting the job done!" They are *meaningful* places to belong. They offer a great sense of purpose but can lack relational warmth.

Then there are churches whose prominent attribute is spiritual passion. Their worship is awe-inspiring. They are *exciting* places to belong. The zeal is undeniable! But that same church may lack strength in the area of the study of the Scriptures or service.

And then there are the quiet liturgical churches. It would be shocking if someone were to utter a spontaneous "amen" in this kind of church. I know. I grew up in one. They are *reliable and comfortable* places to belong. Yet their traditional ways may make them ineffective at relating to and reaching the lost within their surrounding community.

THE MISSION OF THE CHURCH: MAKING DISCIPLES

Each church group tends to defend its distinctive expression of community as a superior reflection of the priorities of Scripture. Said another way, "My church is better than your church." Dietrich Bonhoeffer reminds us that the church is not held together by ideals, styles or a particular vision. He states, "Christian brotherhood is not an ideal which we must realize; it is rather a reality created by God in Christ in which we may participate."[1] Bonhoeffer confronted every attempt at artificiality—that is, manmade trappings that confuse the true basis of Christian community. He goes on, "The man who fashions a visionary ideal of community demands that it be realized by God, by others, and by himself."[2] Demanding anything from God is not a good strategy for making progress. We do well to recall that the church is Christ's, not ours. We do not get to pick its essential purposes.

Bonhoeffer went on to offer this poignant observation: "The more clearly we learn to recognize that the ground and strength and promise of all our fellowship is in Jesus Christ alone, the more serenely shall we think of our fellowship and pray and hope for it."[3] Once we strip away all of the secondary differences, we see the church as it is—a collection of believers who need help in making spiritual progress. This is why a church-wide spiritual assessment is helpful for every kind of church.

There are as many comparisons about the spiritual makeup of churches as there are about the spiritual conditions of individuals. The same kind of observations could be made about denominations. Many have rallying points and work hard to emphasize their distinctive traits from other circles of Faith. The primary issue is not our distinctive doctrines and practices. The real question is, "How effective are we at helping people to grow in Christ?"

Why do we expend so much energy on secondary matters when the primary mission is so urgent and demanding? Part of the answer has to do with lack of clarity about how God grows people. Leaders do not know where to start so they focus on the things they know.

THE NEED FOR CLARITY IN THE CHURCH

There is universal recognition in Christendom that a person is justified by faith in Christ. Beyond that, there are no widely accepted, compelling concepts of where to go from there and what it looks like once we arrive. What does it mean to be spiritually mature?

Ask the average pastor, "What is your plan to grow the people under your care?" Often you will get a blank stare. Others will rattle off a list of courses offered by their church or tout their small groups as a cure-all. The most common approach seems like a version of the old adage, "Throw a lot of mud at the wall and hope enough sticks to make a difference." Even the best of these efforts still lack any measurable means to determine success or failure.

There is a substantial body of biblical evidence that a congregational spiritual assessment is not only possible but also needed. Many of the New Testament epistles were directed to churches whose spiritual issues largely defined the spiritual condition of the entire congregation. The most striking examples are seven letters located at the beginning of the book of Revelation. It makes one wonder: What kind of letter would Jesus write to my church? Do we need one any less than they needed one?

Jesus utilized a consistent process when he addressed these churches. He began by praising them for their strengths. This is a great place to start! Every healthy church needs to know and celebrate its strengths. It builds morale.

Then he confronted their growth areas. Every church has growth areas. Congregants are done a disservice if the pastor only talks about how wonderful they are all the time. Every church and every person needs to be spiritually challenged to press on to achieve the high calling of Christ.

A JESUS-STYLE CHURCH ASSESSMENT

Let's look at how Jesus diagnosed two of the seven churches.

Jesus diagnosed the church at Ephesus as a *love-deficient church* that had "left their first love" (Revelation 2:4). The church at Laodicia was a *deeds-deficient church*. "I know your deeds" (Revelation 3:15). Below is the typical process that Jesus used to promote the spiritual advancement of these churches.

1. A diagnosis: where you are

2. A prognosis: where you are going (without treatment)

3. A treatment plan: what to do

Let's dig deeper and see how this process was specifically applied to the church at Laodecia. This same analysis can be done for every one of the seven churches.

Diagnosis: Lukewarm. "I know your deeds, that you are neither cold nor hot" (Revelation 3:15). They were so distracted by prosperity and the momentary attractions of the world that they lost their zeal for God and his kingdom. Does this sound like any church you know? According to the spiritual growth model of this book, this is a church that would be diagnosed as low in Faith and Hope. Literally, in the Greek, they boasted, "I am rich and I have gotten riches."[4]

Materialism is one of the mortal enemies of Faith and Hope. It is easy for a financially prosperous church to deceive itself into thinking it is spiritually on track. But for Laodecia, their behavioral symptoms told a far different story than the one they imagined. Jesus called them on it. Faith-filled and Hope-filled churches are, by nature, beehives of kingdom activity. They cannot help themselves. They have been captured and captivated by the goodness of God and the promises of a glorious eternal future. They are motivated to serve.

Prognosis: Further rejection and decline. "So because you are lukewarm . . . I will spit you out of My mouth" (Revelation 3:16). Things are not looking good here without some repentance and change. We do well to remember that the long-term consequences of spiritual stagnation can be very severe.

Prescribed treatment. Three cures are offered.

1. Refocusing and investing in heavenly treasures—"true riches"[5]

2. Repentance and cleansing

3. Fresh anointing

"I advise you to buy from Me gold refined by fire so that you may become rich, and white garments so that you may clothe yourself, and that the shame of your nakedness will not be revealed; and eye salve to anoint your eyes so that you may see" (Revelation 3:18).

Jesus closed out this letter with an explanation of his heart: "Those whom I love, I reprove and discipline; therefore be zealous and repent" (Revelation 3:19). Spiritual assessments have no value if they are not focused on making a better future. There is hope for the recovery of this church. Spiritual progress is always the only reason for submitting to the exercise of a spiritual assessment.

A CALL TO THE CHURCH

This book is a call for the restoration of the virtues to their appropriate preeminent role in spiritual progress. The church needs nothing less than a renaissance in how it grows people. The motivational powers of Faith, Hope and Love represent a solid foundation for this crucial mission. Our ways have not worked. We need to go God's way.

The decline of the church and its influence in the United States is well documented. A recent op-ed article in the Sunday edition of the *New York Times* noted, "In 2011 the Pew Forum on Religion and Public Life polled church leaders from around the world. Evangelical ministers from the United States reported a greater loss of influence than church leaders from any other country—with some 82 percent indicating that their movement was losing ground."[6]

The path to restored spiritual power and influence will require the emergence of multitudes of transformed individuals into the market-place. Where will they come from? The church must help produce them. It must learn how to do a better job of growing spiritually powerful people. This is the one observable product of the church. Mediocrity will not do. Changed lives are the light on the hill that Jesus spoke about. Only spiritually powerful people with transformed character can consistently shine in this way. "Let your light shine before men in such a way that they may see your good works, and glorify your Father who is in heaven" (Matthew 5:16). Success is achievable when we join God's way instead of trying to convince him to make our ways work.

THE VALUE OF CHURCH-WIDE ASSESSMENTS

Anonymity is an enemy of spiritual progress. The modern pastor needs all the information they can get, to effectively know and lead their flock to spiritual growth. A church assessment empowers church leaders to make informed decisions and interventions based on the actual growth needs of their congregation by revealing new and useful information, like

- The church's level of Faith, Hope and Love
- The top three character traits in both strength and growth areas
- The most intense spiritual balances or imbalances
- Concrete metrics on the spiritual progress of different ministries within a single church
- Year-to-year comparisons of spiritual progress

SpiritualProgress.com provides online character assessments, cus-tomized growth plans, individual online courses, downloadable small group courses, personal life coaching and online learning opportu-nities. Growth plans are pushed to computers and mobile devices, including smartphones and Apple and Google apps (so you can grow wherever you are). Growth plans include daily audio devotionals that specifically target your greatest growth areas. Personal life coaches are available to speak with you and help guide you on your journey. There is a solid and extensive biblical foundation behind everything that we do.

The six principles below identify the biblical priorities behind the growth plans at SpiritualProgress.com.

1. Broadcast God's Word: Most people are too busy to sit down and absorb personal growth materials on a regular basis. That's why we push our growth content to computers and mobile devices. We are in the midst of a mobile revolution. Everywhere you look you see smartphones and earbuds. We use cutting-edge technology to bring the wisdom of the ages to you wherever you are.

2. Target points of personal need: We need to maximize our time and know that the content that we are receiving is designed to have a maximal impact on our spiritual progress. Our growth content targets your greatest needs, as revealed by your personal online assessment.

3. Frequency: It is not quantity but frequency that makes the biggest impact on our spiritual progress. The ancient Israelites learned this during their forty-year sojourn through the desert. Manna, the bread from heaven, is delivered daily, and it must be consumed fresh.

4. Digestible-sized portions: God's Word is powerful. A very small amount that speaks to our present need can have a huge impact on our lives. It is so rich in content that a person can only truly absorb a small portion at a time.

5. Focus on motivations: Spiritual progress is not about endlessly chasing bad behaviors (symptoms) in a constant quest to change them. Real progress requires that we penetrate down to the level of our motivations (root causes).

6. Live the Word: It is not enough to be a hearer of the Word. We need to be moved to the point of becoming a doer. Each growth plan session concludes with a practical character exercise for the day. This requires that a person "Live the Word" by applying it daily to his or her life.

FINAL THOUGHTS

The biblical foundations that have been laid in this book provide a road map for making spiritual progress. This map helps us to see an invisible, spiritual realm. It is a land filled with surging currents of positive and negative motivations. There are towering mountains of temptation, green pastures of rest and fresh streams of inspiration. It is a spiritual landscape, upon which we are called to successfully navigate and prevail.

The objective of spiritual progress is always to become more Christlike in our character. We are in the process of regaining all that Adam and Eve lost through their rebellion in the Garden. As we become more like Jesus, who is called the second Adam, we become more fully human. Call it a homecoming.

God has bigger plans for you than to arrive in heaven as a broken, dysfunctional soul. He is the ultimate high-end restoration specialist. God is at work to make us a testimony of his transforming power. All we need to do is to cooperate with him in his Spirit-powered mission to grow us. May the Spirit cause you to grow up into the full maturity of character that fulfills every desire of your heart, impacts everyone around you and glorifies God.

Appendix A

14 PRINCIPLES FOR GROWING IN FAITH

Below are some principles that are worthy of significant reflection. If you read and meditate on them regularly, they will help you to grow in Faith.

1. **The Determination Principle**—Faith presses in. "If I only touch His garment, I will get well" (Matthew 9:21).

2. **The Humility Principle**—Faith is not presumption. "Think so as to have sound judgment, as God has allotted to each a measure of faith" (Romans 12:3).

3. **The Invisibility Principle**—Faith overcomes visible circumstances. "For we walk by faith, not by sight" (2 Corinthians 5:7).

4. **The Self-Examination Principle**—Faith needs to be periodically evaluated. "Test yourselves to see if you are in the faith; examine yourselves!" (2 Corinthians 13:5).

5. **The Adoption Principle**—Faith is about being a child. "For you are all sons of God through faith in Christ Jesus" (Galatians 3:26).

6. **The Love Principle**—Faith is a sister to love. "For in Christ Jesus [nothing] means anything, but faith working through love" (Galatians 5:6).

7. **The Warfare Principle**—Faith stops spiritual attacks. "In addition to all, [take] up the shield of faith with which you will be able to extinguish all the flaming arrows of the evil one" (Ephesians 6:16).

8. **The Intimacy Principle**—Faith clings to God. "Let us draw near with a sincere heart in full assurance of faith" (Hebrews 10:22).

9. **The Source Principle**—Faith always looks to Jesus. "[Let us fix] our eyes on Jesus, the author and perfecter of faith" (Hebrews 12:2).

10. **The Testing Principle**—Faith grows stronger when tested. "The testing of your faith produces endurance" (James 1:3).

11. **The Confidence Principle**—Faith entertains no doubts. "But he must ask in faith without any doubting" (James 1:6).

12. **The Verification Principle**—Faith is proven by actions. "Even so faith, if it has no works, is dead, being by itself" (James 2:17).

13. **The Power Prayer Principle**—Faith prays boldly. "The prayer offered in faith will restore the one who is sick" (James 5:15).

14. **The Victory Principle**—Faith makes us overcomers. "Whatever is born of God overcomes the world; and this is the victory that has overcome the world—our faith" (1 John 5:4).

Appendix B

14 PRINCIPLES FOR GROWING IN HOPE

Below are some principles that are worthy of significant reflection. If you read and meditate on them regularly, they will help you to grow in Hope.

1. **The Invisibility Principle**—Hope sees the unseeable. "Hope that is seen is not hope; for who hopes for what he already sees?" (Romans 8:24).

2. **The Joy Principle**—Hope is full of joy. "Be joyful in hope" (Romans 12:12 NIV).

3. **The Investment Principle**—Hope makes eternal deposits. "The plowman ought to plow in hope, and the thresher to thresh in hope of sharing the crops" (1 Corinthians 9:10).

4. **The Confidence Principle**—Hope speaks boldly. "Therefore having such a hope, we use great boldness in our speech" (2 Corinthians 3:12).

5. **The Eternity Principle**—Hope is tied to the future. "If we have hoped in Christ in this life only, we are of all men most to be pitied" (1 Corinthians 15:19).

6. **The Endurance Principle**—Hope must be firmly grasped. "Con-

tinue in the faith firmly established and steadfast, and not moved away from the hope of the gospel" (Colossians 1:23).

7. **The Tough Guy Principle**—Hope loves a challenge. "We also exult in our tribulations, knowing that tribulation brings about perseverance; and perseverance . . . hope" (Romans 5:3-4).

8. **The Indwelling Principle**—Christ brings hope. "Christ in you, the hope of glory" (Colossians 1:27).

9. **The Work Ethic Principle**—Hope sees the reward in every challenge. "It is for this we labor and strive, because we have fixed our hope on the living God" (1 Timothy 4:10).

10. **The Protection Principle**—Hope guards our minds against despair. "[Put on] as a helmet, the hope of salvation" (1 Thessalonians 5:8).

11. **The Expectation Principle**—Hope has a sense of immediacy. "[We look] for the blessed hope and the appearing of the glory of our great God and Savior, Christ Jesus" (Titus 2:13).

12. **The Anchor Principle**—Hope provides strong moorings. "This hope we have as an anchor of the soul, a hope both sure and steadfast" (Hebrews 6:19).

13. **The Purification Principle**—Hope expunges impure motivations. "Everyone who has this hope fixed on Him purifies himself, just as He is pure" (1 John 3:3).

14. **The Evangelism Principle**—Hope demands to be shared with others. "Who is our hope or joy or crown of exultation? Is it not even you, in the presence of our Lord Jesus at His coming?" (1 Thessalonians 2:19).

Appendix C

14 PRINCIPLES FOR GROWING IN LOVE

Below are some principles that are worthy of significant reflection. If you read and meditate on them regularly, they will help you to grow in Love.

1. **The Overriding Principle**—Love must guide every action. "Let all that you do be done in love" (1 Corinthians 16:14).

2. **The Generosity Principle**—Love gives rather than takes. "Walk in love, just as Christ also loved you and gave Himself up for us" (Ephesians 5:2).

3. **The Empathy Principle**—Love enables you to put yourself in the place of another. "If there is any other commandment, it is summed up in this saying, 'You shall love your neighbor as yourself'" (Romans 13:9).

4. **The Power Principle**—Love is the greatest moral force in the universe. "We are more than conquerors through him who loved us" (Romans 8:37 NIV).

5. **The Initiatory Principle**—Love is not passive but takes initiative. "Be devoted to one another in brotherly love" (Romans 12:10).

6. **The Motivational Principle**—Love inspires associated virtuous behaviors. "The love of Christ controls us" (2 Corinthians 5:14).

7. **The Growth Principle** — Everyone needs to grow in love. "This I pray, that your love may abound still more and more" (Philippians 1:9).

8. **The Illumination Principle** — Love enlightens the soul. "The one who loves his brother abides in the Light" (1 John 2:10).

9. **The Primacy Principle** — Love's source is God. "We love, because He first loved us" (1 John 4:19).

10. **The Abiding Principle** — Love is sustained in relationship with God. "Keep yourselves in the love of God" (Jude 21).

11. **The Acceptance Principle** — Love celebrates God's unconditional love. "There is no fear in love; but perfect love casts out fear" (1 John 4:18).

12. **The Liberty Principle** — Love frees us from all guilt. "Love covers a multitude of sins" (1 Peter 4:8).

13. **The Obedience Principle** — Love obeys God. "This is the love of God, that we keep His commandments" (1 John 5:3).

14. **The Purification Principle** — Sincere love requires purification. "Since you have in obedience to the truth purified your souls for a sincere love of the brethren, fervently love one another from the heart" (1 Peter 1:22).

ACKNOWLEDGMENTS

This book has been twenty-five years in the writing. A great many friends and family have helped me along the way.

First and foremost, many thanks are due to my wife and soul mate, Sherrie, who always encouraged the dream, put up with a great many late nights and dared to give me countless hours of straightforward feedback. To the extent that this book is an easy read, she is chiefly responsible.

I have a compelling need to thank my life-long friend Matt Gruver, who kept the faith and patiently walked with me through many renditions of copy to get to this final form.

I also want to thank Gary Morefield, my brother-in-law, whose prophetic response twenty-five years ago ignited a fire in me that kept burning through the many ensuing years.

I owe a debt to Charlie Bradshaw, who came alongside me during my darkest hours and encouraged me to pursue the unchangeable purposes of God.

Many thanks go to Hal Seed, who connected me with my publisher, encouraged me and dared to be the first pilot church for the sermons and small group materials that apply the principles in this book.

The same thanks go to Barry Sappington, whose unflagging positive spirit and faith in the principles of this book led him to open his church as our second pilot church.

I also want to thank Larry Osborne, whose faith and encouragement helped me to make it to the finish line.

NOTES

Chapter Two: The Three Great Forces of Positive Motivation

[1]Thomas Aquinas, *A Shorter Summa* (Manchester, NH: Sophia Institute Press, 1993), p. 4.

[2]Augustine, quoted in ibid.

[3]Gerhard Kittel, ed., *Theological Dictionary of the New Testament* (Grand Rapids: Eerdmans, 1964), 2:635.

[4]Ibid., 3:827, 829.

[5]Walter Bauer, William Arndt and F. Wilbur Gingrich, *A Greek-English Lexicon of the New Testament and Early Christian Literature* (Chicago: University of Chicago Press, 1957), p. 854.

[6]Gordon Fee, *God's Empowering Presence* (Peabody, MA: Hendrickson Publishers, 1994), p. 212.

Chapter Three: The Three Great Isms That Rule the World

[1]"Egotism," http://en.wikipedia.org/wiki/Egotism#cite_ref-1.

[2]"Hedonism," www.thefreedictionary.com/hedonism.

[3]Marvin Bittinger, "The Paradox of Materialism vs. Spirituality," http://christianityandscience.over-blog.com.

[4]www.pickthebrain.com/blog/what-is-eq-and-why-should-you-care/.

[5]"Hedonism," http://en.wikipedia.org/wiki/Hedonism.

[6]This is a research list compiled by Safe Families: www.safefamilies.org/sfStats.php.

[7]Marriage stats can be found at http://postmasculine.com/infidelity-statistics.

[8]Internet Filter Review: http://internet-filter-review.toptenreviews.com/internet-pornography-statistics.html.

[9]Safe Families, www.safefamilies.org/sfStats.php.

[10]Internet Filter Review: http://internet-filter-review.toptenreviews.com/internet-pornography-statistics.html.

[11]This is the second definition for *materialism* at the Free Dictionary: www.thefreedictionary.com/materialistic.

[12]Carey Goldberg, "Materialism Is Bad for You, Studies Say," *International Herald Tribune*, February 9, 2006.
[13]Ibid.
[14]"Consumption and Consumerism," www.globalissues.org/issue/235/consumption-and-consumerism.
[15]"Egotism," www.vocabulary.com/dictionary/egotism.
[16]"Ego," www.vocabulary.com/dictionary/ego.
[17]Sean Keener, "Signs of an Over-Inflated Ego," http://sean.keener.org/things-to-remember/signs-of-an-over-inflated-ego.html.
[18]Ibid.

Chapter Four: The Balances of Motivation

[1]Jerry Bridges, *The Pursuit of Holiness* (Colorado Springs: NavPress, 2006), p. 16.
[2]Henry Blackaby, *Experiencing God* (Nashville: Broadman and Holman, 1998), p. 19.
[3]Dallas Willard and Don Simpson, *Revolution of Our Character* (Colorado Springs: NavPress, 2005), p. 11.

Chapter Five: Motivational Exercise

[1]Dallas Willard, *The Spirit of the Disciplines* (San Francisco: Harper & Row, 1988), p. 19.
[2]Ibid., p. 137.
[3]James Houston, *The Transforming Friendship* (Oxford: Lion, 1989), p. 140.
[4]Dallas Willard and Don Simpson, *Revolution of Our Character* (Colorado Springs: NavPress, 2005), p. 126.
[5]We have used the terms *heart* and *spirit* interchangeably throughout this chapter. Willard notes that the biblical evidence supports that "'heart,' 'spirit' and 'will' are words that refer to one and the same thing." Dallas Willard, *Renovation of the Heart* (Colorado Springs: NavPress, 2002), p. 29.
[6]Richard Foster, *Celebration of Discipline* (San Francisco: Harper & Row, 1978) The table of contents is structured according to the inward, outward and corporate spiritual disciplines. It is a classic read on the spiritual disciplines and their impact on spiritual growth.
[7]Willard, *Spirit of the Disciplines*, p. 175.
[8]Ibid., p. 158.
[9]John Ortberg, *The Life You've Always Wanted* (Grand Rapids: Zondervan, 2002), p. 45.
[10]Richard Foster, *Life with God* (New York: HarperOne, 2008), p. 140.
[11]Ortberg, *The Life You've Always Wanted*, p. 53.
[12]A. W. Tozer, *The Pursuit of God* (Camp Hill, PA: Wingspread Publishers, 2006), p. 61.

Chapter Six: Changing Your Tree

[1]Mike Wall, "World's Largest Atom Smasher May Have Detected 'God Particle,'" www.foxnews.com/scitech/2011/04/22/worlds-largest-atom-smasher-detected -god-particle/.

[2]J. I. Packer, *Knowing God* (Downers Grove, IL: InterVarsity Press, 1973), p. 67.

[3]Ibid., p. 66.

[4]"No single word can provide an adequate rendering. . . . 'Supporter' or 'helper' is perhaps the best, though the basic concept and sustaining religious idea is that of 'advocate.'" Gerhard Kittel, ed., *Theological Dictionary of the New Testament* (Grand Rapids: Eerdmans, 1964), 5:814.

[5]James Houston, *The Transforming Friendship* (Oxford: Lion, 1989), p. 136.

[6]Dallas Willard and Don Simpson, *Revolution of Our Character* (Colorado Springs: NavPress, 2005), p. 16.

[7]Rick Warren, *The Purpose Driven Life* (Grand Rapids: Zondervan, 2002), p. 186. Warren goes on to state, "God's Word generates faith, produces change, frightens the Devil, causes miracles, heals hurts, builds character, transforms circumstances, imparts joy, overcomes adversity, defeats temptation infuses hope, releases power, cleanses our minds, brings things into being, and guarantees our future forever!"

[8]"There is absolutely no shortcut to holiness that bypasses or gives little priority to a consistent intake of the Bible." Jerry Bridges, *The Pursuit of Holiness* (Colorado Springs: NavPress, 2006), p. 109.

Chapter Seven: Faith

[1]"Nuclear Weapons—Development of Nuclear Weapons," http://science.jrank .org/pages/4758/Nuclear-Weapons-Development-nuclear-weapons.html.

[2]"The Atom Bomb," www.century-of-flight.net/Aviation%20history/WW2 /atom%20bomb.htm.

Chapter Eleven: Love

[1]Four squads of four soldiers were dispatched to guard Peter. How much more of a perceived threat was possible from a backlash of Jesus' followers? There were at least sixteen guarding his tomb.

[2]In prebiblical Greek times, "The verb is often used to denote regard or friendship between equals, or sometimes sympathy." Jesus uses ἀγάπη [*agapē*] in a far different way. "By His act of forgiveness God has instituted for humanity a new order which supersedes the old worldly order of rank. . . . The new relationship of God to man lays the foundation of a new relationship of man to man." Gerhard Kittel, ed., *Theological Dictionary of the New Testament* (Eerdmans, 1964), 1:36, 47.

[3]"It brings out more clearly what is at issue in Lk. 7:47, namely, that a new life has awakened and the person now has love, is filled with it, and is guided by it in all his actions." Ibid., 1:47.

[4]Servais Pinckaers, *The Sources of Christian Ethics* (Washington, DC: Catholic University of America Press, 1995), p. 27.

[5]"Always where the interrelationship of the three is given with any precision, the emphasis falls wholly on ἀγάπη [*agapē*]. . . . Ἀγάπη [*agapē*] stands under the sign of the τέλος [*telos*]. This is the great truth of 1 C. 13." Kittel, *Theological Dictionary of the New Testament*, 1:51.

Chapter Twelve: The Distortions of Love

[1]Mark Twain, *Notebook of 1898*, www.twainquotes.com/Christianity.html.

Chapter Thirteen: Growing Forward

[1]Dietrich Bonhoeffer, *Life Together* (New York: Harper, 1954), p. 30.

[2]Ibid., p. 27.

[3]Ibid., p. 30.

[4]George Ladd, *A Commentary on the Revelation of John* (Grand Rapids: Eerdmans, 1972), p. 66.

[5]Ibid. "In the present verse, Christ exhorts the church to secure for herself the true riches—gold refined by fire which will not tarnish."

[6]John S. Dickerson, "The Decline of Evangelical America," *New York Times*, December 15, 2012, www.nytimes.com/2012/12/16/opinion/sunday/the-decline -of-evangelical-america.html?pagewanted=all&_r=0.